THE LEGACY, THE TESTAMENT, AND OTHER POEMS OF FRANÇOIS VILLON

THE LEGACY, THE TESTAMENT, AND OTHER POEMS

OF

FRANÇOIS VILLON

TRANSLATED BY

PETER DALE

ST. MARTIN'S PRESS

 For information, write:
St. Martin's Press, Inc., 175 Fifth Ave.,
New York, N.Y. 10010
Printed in Great Britain
Library of Congress Catalog Card Number: 72–85557
First Published in the United States of America in 1973

Affiliated Publishers: Macmillan Limited, London—
also at Bombay, Calcutta, Madras and Melbourne

FOR
WILLIAM COOKSON

Illustrations by
MICHAEL DENNING

A NOTE ON THE TRANSLATION

'Strict metrical translators still exist. They seem to live in a world untouched by contemporary poetry. Their difficulties are bold and honest, but they are taxidermists, not poets, and their poems are likely to be stuffed birds. . . .' So wrote Robert Lowell in his introduction to *Imitations*.

This translation is a strict metrical translation and would seem, from Lowell's remarks, to require justification in modern eyes. It seems to me that to translate a very formal poet into free verse is as odd as to attempt to translate *The Cantos* into heroic couplets. Traffic in either direction is as illogical. The fact is that the exigencies of form that the translator faces are more or less the same as the author faced – and these are part of the texture of the poem. Lowell goes on to recognise this in his introduction: 'A better strategy would seem to be the now fashionable translations into free or irregular verse. Yet this method commonly turns out a sprawl of language, neither faithful nor distinguished, now on stilts, now low, as Dryden would say.' Lowell himself opts for a half way house: 'I believe that poetic translation – I would call it an imitation – must be expert and inspired, and needs at least as much technique, luck and rightness of hand as an original poem.'

In his practice with Villon, he has fallen between two stools by neither adhering to the strict rhyme-scheme to establish expectancy and rhyme-compulsion nor discarding rhyme altogether:

> Who cares then to die shriven?
> Feet cramp, the nostrils curve,
> eyes stare, the stretched veins hiss
> and ache through joint and nerve –

The gist of this is in the original, except 'nostrils curve' which is clearly rhyme-compulsion with no rhyme-scheme to impose it – nor does it add poetry to an otherwise prosaic verse.

My practice has been to use Villon's own ballade stanza as exactly as possible and, like him, to use all the devices of change of tone, exclamation, and seeming irrelevance to master the form. The task is somewhat more difficult in English because of the lack of rhyme-words not to mention Villon's remarkable skill in rhyming on the exact word, as Pound pointed out.

So much for generalities. It remains true that Villon cannot really be translated; he can only be dislocated. He has muscle and he has music, a mastery of form. In English translation, you cannot convincingly and consistently have all three. I have tried to articulate muscle and bones, the sleight of mood – the music has had to make shift for itself. A ghost of it lingers, I hope, in the more straightforward stanzas.

In a verse translation you cannot always render what a man is saying; you must translate his way of saying. The exigencies of rhyme, idiom, pun and innuendo lead Villon to certain nonchalances of expression and a cavalier attitude to form that cannot always occur at the same point in a language of different idioms and greater problems in rhyme. For example, in the middle section of *The Legacy* with its knockabout humour, I have used the occasional Hudibrastic rhyme which clearly conveys the mood in English though there is no equivalent in French with its different rhyme-system.

Villon's subject has further created more localised problems. The will-form requires that phrases like 'I give'; 'I bequeath'; 'I leave' regularly open stanzas. They are awkward rhyme words in English so a degree of inversion is required. (The original is not without inversion.) This problem is deepened by the fact that things are left to proper names, which, being French, have to be kept from the end of the line or anglicised.

So much for the letter; it is the spirit one needs to translate. Apart from the formal challenge, what interested me was Villon's voice, the paradoxical moods he controls: the nonchalant concern; the sad gaiety; the gallows humour; the arrogant humility (and vice-versa); the comic pathos – the energy, verve and the sheer music.

No version of Villon can satisfy for long. If this one opens again the possibility of strict metrical translation it will have lasted long enough.

If it does, William Cookson, who encouraged me in the project and supplied many texts I have used, must take chief credit.

I am equally indebted to the versions of Anthony Bonner of *Complete Works of François Villon* (Museum Press: London: 1960) and to Galway Kinnell's versions in *The Poems of François Villon* (Signet Classic: 1965). Swinburne's, Lowell's, Wilbur's, and most of all, Tom Scott's versions have been of great assistance in deciding what one may or may not get away with in a verse translation.

Peter Dale

A BIOGRAPHICAL NOTE ON VILLON

François Villon was born François Montcorbier or François des Loges in Paris in 1431. He took his surname, Villon, from his guardian and benefactor, Guillaume de Villon, chaplain of Saint Benoît-le-Bétourné, a man of whom he speaks well in both *The Legacy* and *The Testament*. He took his baccalauréat from the University of Paris in 1449. Around 1451, he was probably involved in a student rag which removed a landmark (le Pet au Diable: The Devil's Fart) from the front of Mademoiselle de Bruyère's house. He, himself, mentions a poem, *The Romance of the Devil's Fart*, in *the Testament*. However, in 1452, he received his *licence* and *maître ès arts* from the University of Paris. His first clash with the law occurred in 1455 when he was involved in a fight with a priest who was killed. An eye-witness, admittedly a friend of Villon's, maintains that he acted in self-defence. Though pardoned for the murder in 1456, that same year he was implicated in the famous robbery of five-hundred golden *écus* from the College of Navarre. Guy Tabary and Colin de Cayeux are two of his confederates mentioned in *The Testament*. In this year he wrote, presumably in some haste, *The Legacy*. Tabary's confession to the robbery in 1457, made Villon leave Paris and go on the run. Much of the rest of the detail of his life comes from *The Testament* on the assumption that it is truly autobiographical. According to this he was imprisoned, somewhat unjustly or pettily if his mood is anything to judge from, by the Bishop of Orléans in his palace-dungeons at Meung. He was set free to celebrate King Louis XI's progress through the town. In this year he wrote *The Testament* in which he speaks of wanderings and various towns that must have been his itinerary between, say, 1456 and 1461. In 1462, he is again in prison, The Châtelet, charged with the robbery of the College of Navarre. The church was more interested in cash than crime and he was released quickly on promising to repay the money taken or at least his cut. The last real fact we have about Villon was his arrest for brawling later in 1462. Although he seems to have been a mere onlooker he was sentenced to death. Parliament set aside the sentence, imposing banishment from Paris. Villon vanishes from history at this point, aged thirty-two.

THE LEGACY

I.

Fourteen fifty-six was the year
when I, François Villon by name,
a scholar, mind and senses clear,
champing the bit and feeling game,
knowing that one must judge one's fame
and works as Vegetius truly states,
wise Roman, counsellor without blame,
or otherwise one miscalculates . . .[1]

2.

At this time as I said before,
the Christmas-tide, the dead season,
when wolves live off the wind and poor
people stay at home with reason
and burn up logs in fear of freezing,
desire came strong to have me start
and make a break for total freedom:[2]
the cell of love would crack my heart.

3.

And so I did it in this way,
seeing her always before me go,
permitting my destruction, day
by day, no happier for it though.

F W

1 4 5 6

I grieve to heaven that this is so,
and pray for vengeance from the gods
of love, and plead again they show
mercy on those that love at odds.

4.

I took it all as in my favour:
fine appearances, soft glance,
but double-crossing her behaviour,
she tortured me on my own lance.
She savaged me, and not by chance
she showed so clean a pair of heels.
In my great need she would not answer:
I must go plough in other fields.[3]

5.

The eyes of her had taken me,
she who had double-crossed me so.
I'd done no harm that I could see
and yet her wish commands I go
to death and be no more. I know
there's little I can do but leave.
She'd cut me dead with a single blow
and never hear my last words heave.

6.

It would, I think, be wise to go
and dodge these dangers now. Goodbye,

I'm off to Angers. She gives me no
favour, not a bit.[4] I die
in her though sound in health. Yet I,
the martyred lover, rise above
all this and I'll be counted high
numbered among the Saints of Love.

7.

However hard it comes, I must
now leave her to it. My dim wit
conceives that someone else has thrust
his shuttle in and out a bit.
No Boulogne kipper on the spit
dried out of humour more than me.
A sorry business, all of it.
– Pray God may hear my misery.

8.

And since I now must leave my place
and lack assurance of return
(I'm not a man without a trace
of blame, nor made of stuff more stern
than most, no iron or steel concern),
since human life's uncertain still
and death no rescue, since I yearn
for a far country, I make my will.

9.

Now in the name of Father, Son,
the Holy Ghost and our Lady's Grace
that leaves no soul for lost, not one,
I leave (D.V.) in pride of place
my fame that rumour yet may trace
back to the honour of his name
to Guillaume Villon; in any case,
my tents and pavilion to the same.

10.

Item: to the lady mentioned above
who overturned my applecart
and drove me from the joys of love,
I leave relictuary[5] my heart,
pale, piteous and dead. Her part
it was that tossed me to this fate
and ruined pleasure for a start:
may God show mercy on her state.

11.

Item: To Ythier Marchant[6] – I feel
obliged to him somehow – or was it
Jean le Cornu? I leave my steel
sword, razor sharp. But no deposit
as it's in pawn. And not to cosset
either of them, I hereby pray
it's given both – only because it's
what they'll ask for if they pay.

12.

Item: to St Amant,[7] *The White Horse*
to make a pair with *The She-Mule*;
and to Blarru[8] I give, of course,
my diamond, that costly jewel,
or bucking *Zebra*. I leave the rule
Omnis utriusque sexus . . .[9] (fence
for the Carmelite bull) to clerics who'll
be stuck enforcing so much sense.

13.

But first and foremost I command
that master Rob Vallée,[10] (a poor
clerk to the parliament who can't
tell hip from whore) receive before
I go my trousers for his whore,
Jeanne de Millières. Though now in hock
down in *The Greaves*, they'll look the more
her style than any kind of frock.

14.

And since his family's well heeled
he must receive more recompense
(The Holy Ghost would have me yield)
because it's clear he's somewhat dense.
It seems to me to make good sense
to give – as cupboards have more brains –
(should Tom Fool manage to dispense
with it) *The Art of Memory*'s remains.

15.

Item: that master Rob may make
himself some sort of livelihood
(and don't be jealous for Christ's sake)
my parents are to get a good
price for my coat of mail and should,
with part, before it's Easter, buy
that mutt a stall and have it stood
beside St Jacques and let him try.

16.

Item: to Jacques Cardon,[11] my friend,
in outright gift I leave my cape
and gloves, and further, at my end,
some willow seed of acorn shape
and every day without escape:
a fleshy goose and capon fat;
ten hogsheads more of chalk than grape;
two briefs. He won't gain much on that!

17.

Item: I leave that noble man
de Montigny,[12] three hounds of mine;
Jean Raguier, all that I can:
a hundred francs I will assign
from all my rents – but draw the line
at any increase with the rents.
Kin shouldn't always buy the wine,
nor friends make up your lost percents.

18.

Item: to Grigny's Lord[13] I give
the watch-tower of Nijon, add
Bicêtre dungeons in which to live,
and six more dogs than Montigny had.
For Mouton, the bastard, nothing's too bad:
three lashes for taking him to court,
and after that he might be glad
to sleep at ease in chains too short.

19.

To Master Raguier,[14] I leave
the Popin Trough, a peach and pear
from the tree of figs. May he receive
the standing choice of titbits there;
that hole *The Pine Cone Inn*, his lair,
where cloaked up like a Jacobin,
secret and close, he'll have his share
and those who plough can get stuck in.

20.

Item: to Jean Mautaint,[15] I give –
to Pierre Basanier, a life share –
their lord's goodwill, so punitive
in prosecuting crime. To wear
during these days of icy air,
I leave my lawyer[16] the leather tights
and caps my cobbler with such flair
tailored according to his lights.

21.

Item: Jean Trouvé,[17] butcher, I leave
The Sheep, so fat and fresh and male;
a cat o' nine tails, he'll receive;
The Horny Ox that's still for sale
and let him knock flies off her tail;
The Cow, if someone gets the bloke
knocking her off on his back. Fail,
and in her harness he will choke.

22.

Item: the Captain of the Watch[18]
I give *The Helmet*. To his men
on foot and groping leg and crotch
along the stalls, I leave them then
a lively larceny, that den
The Lantern in the Stone-milk Lane.
The Lily Pad is mine, though, when
they run me into jail again.

23.

To Perrenet[19] who's widely called
the Bastard of the Bar, I give
three bales of straw to be installed
upon his boards that make one stiff
because his trade's so calmative
and done with love. Or he must beg.
He knows no other way to live
and both require a nifty leg.

24.

Item: to Wolf and Cholet,[20] I wish
to leave a duck poached from the walls
the way we always catch the dish
inside the moat when darkness falls;
to both I grant to hide their hauls
a monkish cloak down to the feet.
My capless boots I give them also,
kindling, charcoal, peas and meat.

25.

Item: and now for pity's sake,
and three small kids all naked there,[21]
(cited below) I hereby make
provision. Orphans in need of care,
shoeless they are, and going bare
as worms. I leave enough to raise
at least a clout or two to spare
and last them through the darkest days.

26.

First, Colin, Girard next, and John,
Goussin, Laurens, Marceau, by birth;
they have no goods, their guardians are gone.
They couldn't raise a bucket's worth.
I parcel them my lands on earth,
or four bob each if they want pay.
Delicate tasters shall cram their girth –
and long before I'm old and grey!

27.

Item: my letters of nomination
had from the University
I leave now by my resignation
to shelter from adversity
poor clerks whose names and quality
I list below. Done, I confess,
in good will and humanity,
seeing them in their nakedness.

28.

Master Guillaume Cotin, and one
Thibaud de Vitry, a pair of poor
latinate clerks of whom there's none
less quarrelsome, nor any more
peaceable – singers who adore
to sing in choir – I leave arrears
of rent on Gueldry's to restore
their wealth till something else appears.

29.

I add to their croziers the crook
from Rue St Antoine, or billiard cues
to cross themselves when off the hook,
and Seine in mugs each day to booze.[22]
I give all those with nothing to lose,
the jailbirds clipped and caged for life,
my mirror's fine, untarnished views
and favours from the jailor's wife.

30.

Item: I leave to hospitals
my cobweb-leaded window panes.[23]
To people lying under stalls,
a black eye each for them remains,
and may they tremble, face all pains,
shivering, unshaven, starved and thin,
frozen and bashed about the brains,
in tatty clothes that soak the skin.

31.

Item: the clippings of my hair,
in full and outright gift, I leave
my barber; and the clothes I wear
the rag-and-bonemen may receive
in the same condition as I leave
them off. My snob I give each shoe
when soleless – my charity achieve
for less than what they cost me new.

32.

Item: I bequeath to wandering Friars,
Beguines, and all the Daughters of God,
dainty titbits (that always inspires)
plump hen, capon, piece of cod,
and custard pies. And then, how odd,
to preach the Fifteen Signs and grub
their bread. What's more, the Carmelite squad
mount on our wives. That's the least rub.

33.

I leave to John the Guard,[24] who deals
in spice, a crutch and *The Golden Mortar*
to help him stand when least he feels
like mixing mustard with his water.
And that bastard who gave no quarter
and wore the hairs out of my head,
St Anthony take him by the shorter.
That's all he'll get when I am dead.

34.

Item: to Merbeuf[25] I bequeath,
and Nick de Louvieux – one each,
an eggshell filled with francs beneath
and crowns on top. And just to teach
a lesson well within his reach,
to Pierre de Rousseville I leave
the paper money, free as speech,
his Prince hands out and fools receive.

35.

And last, while writing this tonight,
in pleasant mood arranging rhyme
and listing all the items right,
I heard the bell of Sorbonne chime.[26]
It always rings that sound at nine:
the Promise of Salvation made.
And so I lingered on this line
and as my heart desired, I prayed.

36.

With this, I must have started dozing
(and not from any wine I'd drunk.)
My mind was half entranced, supposing
I saw Dame Memory open her trunk
and stack on shelves this ancient junk:
dependent species; then came some
opinative; some true, some bunk,
some intellectual, but mostly dumb.[27]

37.

She added those estimative
(by which we prophesy events)
conceptual ones and formative
by which, they say, to all intents
a troubled man might lose his sense
and go insane by the moon's light.
– It's Aristotle, this immense
learning, if memory serve me right.

38.

But then Sensation pulled a wire[28]
and this incited Fantasy
to stir my organs and the higher,
the sovereign part of you and me,
in rigor mortis seemed to be,
oppressed by my forgetfulness –
which then dispersed and came quite free
to prove itself a sense no less.

39.

After my mind had come to rest
my wits began to clear again.
I tried to end the work as best
I could. My ink was frozen then,
the candle blown out God knows when,
and since there was no other light
by which to finish with the pen,
with mittens on, I slept all night.

40.

Signed, sealed and settled on the date
mentioned above by well renowned
Villon who shits no figs or dates,[29]
and like a mop is caked and browned.
Tents and pavilion, while of sound
body and mind, he leaves to friends.
He has in change less than a pound
and that won't last, the way he spends.

THE TESTAMENT

I.

In the thirtieth year of my age
when I had swallowed up my shame,

not wholly foolish, nor yet a sage,
despite the harm and all that came
from Thibault d'Aussigny[1] by name.
Bishop he may be, blessing streets,
but I repudiate the claim
that he is mine, for all his feats.

2.

He's neither lord nor bishop to me.
I had nothing from him but sheer
waste, and return no loyalty.
I'm not his serf or little deer.[2]
He fattened me for half a year
on one small loaf and water free.
Generous? Tight? A sow's ear.
God deal with him as he with me.

3.

If anyone must needs complain
and say I damn the man – not so,
if you can see what I maintain.
I deal in no detraction, though.
Here's all the ill of him I know:
if once he's shown me his compassion,
may Christ, the King of Heaven, show
mercy on him in equal fashion.

4.

Yet if he were so hard on me,
far worse than I can ever tell,
I ask the Lord of Eternity
to deal the like to him as well.
'The Church commands and bids us quell
our hate and pray for all our foes.'
I say I'm wrong and shamed: he fell
on me but under God who knows.

5.

I'll pray for him and with a will
upon the soul of Jean Cotart.
But how? I'm slow at reading still.
In Picard prayers[3] I'll go so far.
He hasn't the faintest what these are
so he must trust I spread no slanders
or go before too late as far
to learn as Lille or Douai in Flanders.

6.

However, he mustn't tell a soul
if he intends to hear my prayer.
I give my word that on the whole
he won't be disappointed there.
When there's a psalter going spare
(not hide- or cordovan-bound) why then
I'll make the seventh verse my prayer
from Deus Laudem[4] and amen.

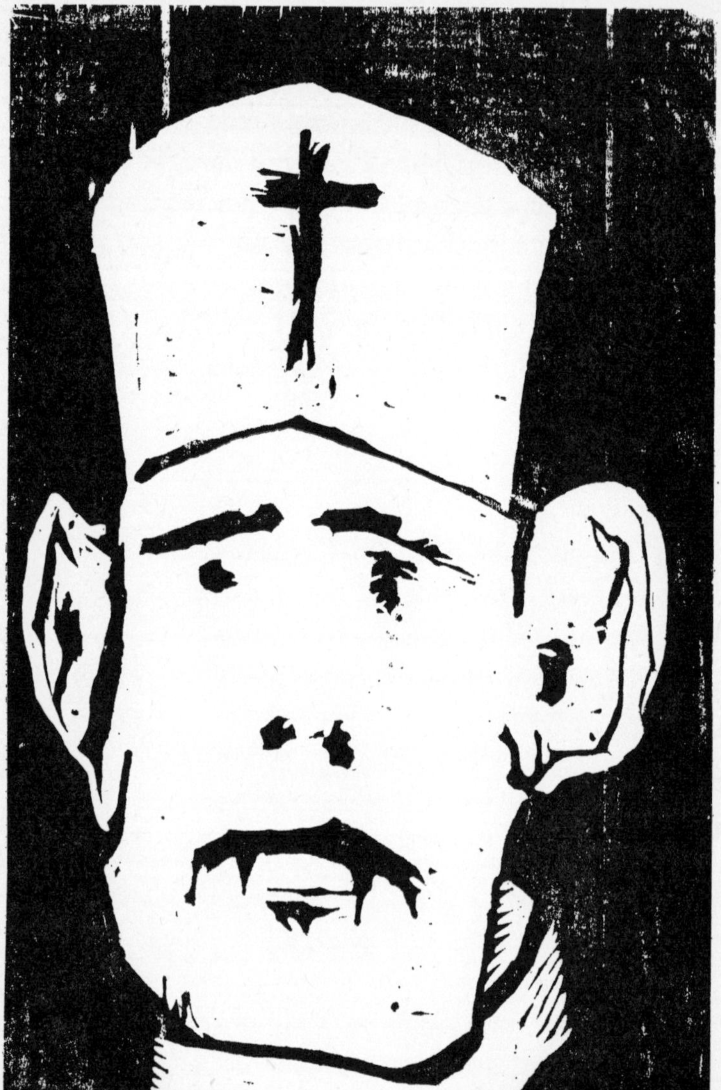

7.

And so I pray the Blessed Son
of God who hears my cries of need
that my poor prayer, all said and done,
find grace with Him from who proceed
body and soul. For I was freed
from wretchedness and vile mischance
and more oppression by God's speed.
Praise Him – and the good King of France.[5]

8.

God grant the King all Jacob's fortune,
the glory and honour of Solomon
(prowess he has in good proportion
and strength of his own to go upon)
and make him such a paragon
throughout the passing world, both near
and far. And so his fame live on,
grant him the years of Methuselah here.

9.

And thus may twelve male children spring
in holy wedlock from his royal line,
and dauntless as great Charles our king,
brave as St Martial[6] was. In fine,
may all his troubles then be tiny
and so may all of these attend
upon the ex-dauphin in time
and Paradise await his end.

10.

And yet, because my strength grows weak,
poorer in goods than in my health,
and while I have the wits to speak
(what few God gave my only wealth
for I've had none by loan or stealth)
I make this will and testament,
the last deposals of myself,
once and for all, my true intent:

11.

Written in sixty one, the year
the King delivered me from jail,
the harsh Meung. When death was near
he gave me life. I shall not fail,
while my heart beats, to tell the tale,
humble myself before the King
and do so till his life shall fail.
Good deeds bear long remembering.

12.

True, that after cries and tears,
and groans of anguish, after pain,
toil and grievous wandering years,
suffering (feelings that remain
as sharp as cottonwool) made plain
more things than Averroës could
in all his Commentaries to explain
what Aristotle understood.

13.

Yet in the depths of my despair
without a penny to my name,
God, who so comforted the pair
of pilgrims to Emmaus, came
and showed me in my deepest shame
a good city filled with great hope.[7]
However vile I was in sin and blame
God hates but those who need more rope.

14.

I am a sinner, I know full well
and yet my death is not God's will,
but my return to live and dwell
in goodness – and others like me still
bitten by sin and doing ill.
However much I die in sin,
God lives and his great mercy will
forgive me if remorse bites in.

15.

Though in those lines right at the start,
the noble *Romance of the Rose*[8]
states that we should excuse young heart
its youth once we have seen it grows
older than old. It's true, God knows!
And that's the reason those that hound
me up and down do not propose
to let my ripe old age come round!

16.

Now if my death would benefit
the common good, as God's my judge,
I would condemn myself for it
and die in sin. I bear no grudge
nor harm for young or old that trudge
the earth on foot or lodge below.
The mountain foot will never budge
for poor men, neither to nor fro.

17.

In Alexander's reign a man,
Diomedes, was brought for trial
before the King and under ban
of death for being beyond denial
the pirate sailing in such style
his men had seen at sea. That's why,
fingers in screws, he stood awhile
to hear the sentence: he must die.

18.

At once the Emperor put the case:
'Why are you a robber on the sea?'
The man answered in the first place:
'Why speak of robber and robbery?
It's just because your men could see
me sail my pirate cockleshell.
If I'd the arms you lead, I'd be
like you – an emperor as well.

19.

'That's how it goes. The life I lead
has come of Fate against whose will
I cannot struggle and succeed.
She casts the lots and cheats me still.
Forgive me for whatever ill
I've done, and learn that beggary –
the common saying fits the bill –
creates so little loyalty.'

20.

The Emperor had understood
Diomedes' defence and swore:
'I'll change your fate from bad to good.'
And did. Diomedes never more
maligned a man, but stood before
them all, honest and worthy too.
Valerian, 'The Great' in Roman lore,
vouches that this tale is true.

21.

Had God allowed my path to cross
an Alexander who could feel
the pity to repair my loss
and I was once more seen to deal
in evil, then without appeal
I would condemn myself to the stake.
It's need that makes men rob and steal;
hunger makes wolves from forests break.

22.

The days of youth I must regret.
I had my fling and more than most,
then came onset of age. And yet
behind my back they seemed to coast
away and not on foot or post,
cavorting, alas, but taking wing.
All of a sudden gone like a ghost
and me stuck here without a thing.

23.

All of them gone and I remain,
poor in my wits and wisdom, sad,
failing, blacker than blue; no gain,
no rents, no property I've had.
My least kin now (it's true, I add)
advance to disown me and forget
the ties of blood. They think it bad,
a lack of change, a length of debt.

24.

I haven't spent it eating well
nor laying women, as they fear.
No excess love has made me sell
a thing to vex my friends with here –
nothing I mean that cost them dear!
On this at least I say, no less,
I'm innocent, my conscience clear.
Who does no wrong need not confess.

25.

Yet it is true that I have loved
and gladly would again, but heart
turned sad and starving gut have shoved
me off the paths of love. My part
is someone else's for a start,
someone whose roast will reach the rafters,
who has the stomach for the tart.
The dance is one for larger grafters.

26.

But in the days of my mad youth
if only I had used my head
and learnt how to behave in truth,
I'd have a house and a soft bed.
But like a naughty boy instead
I ran away from school. I make
these lines and soon as they are said
I feel my heart would almost break.

27.

I took the Sage's words for truth
(much good it did me and to spare)
'Rejoice, oh young man, in thy youth.'[9]
But then again the words declare
another kettle of fish elsewhere:
'Childhood and youth,' to be precise,
no more no less his saying there:
'are vanity, ignorance and vice.'

28.

My days[10] are swiftly spent like ends
the weaver trims off at a stroke
with a burning straw. A thread extends
a bit too far beyond the yoke
and goes up in a puff of smoke;
says Job. So I no longer fear
what twists and turns of fate provoke
for death's the level of all things here.

29.

Where are the lads who cut a dash
I hung on to in earlier days,
in song so fine, in talk so flash,
so taking in their wit and ways?
Some are stark dead. No trace
of them remains. Oh, may they find
in Paradise their peace and place.
God save the others of my kind.

30.

Of these some have become great lords,
thank God, and masters, too. But more
beg naked, their only bread on boards
in shops. And others long before
have entered in the cloister door:
Carthusians or Celestines,[11] no doubt,
and shod for oysterbeds on shore.
The wonder is how men turn out.

31.

God grant great men may do good works
and live the life of peace and quiet.
There's no correcting great men's quirks;
better to belt up than to riot.
The poor have nothing but disquiet,
like me. God grant a patient air!
The others have an ample diet:
rations and bread enough to spare.

32.

Good wines they have and newly broached,
sauces and broths and great fat fish,
custards and tarts, eggs fried or poached
or scrambled – any way they wish.
Nor are they served with every dish
as masons like to be. With wine
they won't have things too waiterish
but pour and drink as they incline.

33.

I've rather wandered off the track
on this digression. No judge to try,
nor one to punish, pardon, rack,
the most imperfect man am I.
Sweet Jesus Christ be praised on high!
And they, through me, the most hard-bitten,
accept his grace before they die.
What I have written, I have written.

34.

Let's leave the Church much where it stands[12]
and talk of far more pleasant things.
No topic everyone expands
on, some it bores and some it brings
annoyance. Poverty always stings
(sad, peevish, lawless, full of spite)
with biting words and murmurings –
and if she daren't, she thinks all right.

35.

From childhood onward I've been poor,
of poor and humble extraction come.
My father never had much store,
grandfather Horace no great sum.
Poverty hounds us from crumb to crumb.
On tombs where my ancestors lie
(God welcome them to Kingdom come!)
no crowns and sceptres catch the eye.

36.

But often when I grouse how poor
my heart butts in and plainly says:
'Come off it, man, now don't deplore
so peevishly that you have less
than Jacques Coeur made.[13] Better to dress
in coarse homespun your skin and bone
than to have left a lord's largesse
and rot beneath the richest stone.'

37.

To have been a lord? What have I said?
The lord's not what he was before.
In David's Psalms it may be read:
'His place shall know of him no more.'
As for the rest, it's not for poor
sinners like me to gloss the text,
but theologians. I leave it for
a preacher to tackle in his next.

38.

I know I'm not, I quite agree,
an angel's son in an aureole
of stars and galaxies, not me.
My father's dead, God rest his soul,
his body in a stone-flagged hole.
My mother's dying, that I know
and she, poor woman, knows the whole.
Nor has her son so far to go.

39.

I know that rich or poor, the wise
or foolish, parishioner or priest,
nobles or peasants, prince and miser,
high or low, beauty or beast,
ladies in high-turned collars, least
and last whatever their conception,
high hat or headscarf, west or east –
Death seizes all without exception.

40.

Though Paris dies and Helen dies,
whoever dies must die in pain:
a hollow in the breath that dries;
spleen bursts upon the heart to drain;
he sweats, my God, he sweats in vain.
For now no brother, sister, son
would take his place and bear that pain
moments before his life is done.

41.

Death trembles him and bleeds him pale,
the nostrils pinch, the veins distend,
the neck is gorged, skin limp and frail.
Joints knot and sinews draw and rend.
O Woman's body, so suave and tender,
so trim and dear, must you arrive
at such an agony in the end?
Oh yes, or rise to Heaven live.

42.

BALLADE.

Now tell me where has Flora gone,[14]
the lovely Roman, her country's where?
Archipiades, Thais that shone,
her cousin once removed? And there
was Echo once, a trace on air,

by ponds and commons she would show
a beauty more than humans bear:
whither the drift of last year's snow?

Where Heloise, whose wisdom shone,
whose love helped Abelard to bear
the gelding he had undergone
when sworn to vows a monk must swear?
And where now is that Queen so fair
who ordered them to sack and throw
Buridan in the Seine down there?
Whither the drift of last year's snow?

Where's Blanche the Queen, white as a swan,
her siren's voice upon the air?
Big-footed Bertha, Beatrice gone;
Alice, and Arembourg once heir
to Maine. Good Joan in Rouen square
burnt by the English. There they go,
but where, O Virgin, tell me where,
whither the drift of last year's snow?

Prince, do not ask in a fortnight where,
nor yet again in a year or so.
This is the burden of the air:
whither the drift of last year's snow?

43.

BALLADE.

And whereabouts is Callixtus the Third,[15]
the last to die descended in that name,

who reignèd three years as pope? And what occurred
to Alphonse, King of Aragon, or became
of Bourbon's gracious Duke? I ask the same
of Arthur, duke of Brittany, and again
with Charles the Seventh of France with all his fame.
But where now is the greatest – Charlemagne?

What of the Scottish King of whom I heard
that half his face was red, or so they claim,
as amethyst from forehead to his beard?
The famous King of Cyprus, what a shame!
and there's that other one, now what's his name?
But I forget now – the good King of Spain!
Where are they gone, the mighty in their fame?
But where now is the greatest – Charlemagne?

I mustn't maunder on. It's so absurd.
The world is nothing but a cheating game.
None can resist death long but is interred
and none can make provision against its claim.
But just one further question all the same:
Ladislaus, King of Bohemia? Then again
where's his grandfather gone from whom he came?
But where now is the greatest – Charlemagne?

And Guesclin's where, that Breton knight of fame?
And Alençon, the brave Duke lately slain?
The Count of the Auvergne, Dauphin by name?
But where now is the greatest – Charlemagne?

44.

BALLADE.[16]

Now whether it's the Saintly Pope
robed in alb and amice, arrayed
in sacred stole and holy cope,
the one who in his anger laid
about the devil – he too must vade
like any knave within his pay.
One gust and light and life must fade:
that much the wind sweeps right away.

Or Emperor of Constantinople,
the golden-fisted – he must fade.
Even the King of France, more noble
than all the other kings, who made
convent and churches all arrayed
in awe of God's great glory. It may
be in his time honour was paid:
that much the wind sweeps right away.

So too the Dauphins of Grenoble,
and Vienne, the wise and brave. Where laid
the Lords of Dijon, Salins? What hope
the Lords of Doles? the sons they made?
And come to that, the whole parade
of heralds, pages, in their pay.
They stuffed their mugs despite their trade:
that much the wind sweeps right away.

Princes for death are also made,
and everyone alive is fey.

Should this rouse anger, I'm afraid
that much the wind sweeps right away.

45.

Since popes and kings and sons of kings
conceived in wombs of queens now lie
stone cold and buried underlings,
their crowns on other heads, won't I,
a poor pedlar from Rennes, just die?
Oh yes, if so it pleases God.
—An honest death would get me by
so long as I have shot my wad.

46.

The world is no abiding place
whatever robber barons think.
All for the chopper in any case.
A comfort this upon the brink
for one who had when in the pink
of youth such wit. Now old and grey,
if he should give a nod and wink
they'd call it filth, senile decay.

47.

And so he has to beg his keep.
Need drags him to this wandering.
Today, tomorrow, he begs for sleep

and death, heartsick with suffering.
And he would do a dreadful thing
but for the fear of God. As it stands
the old do break God's law and bring
about their end with their own hands.

48.

For if when young he had a wit
no sally now can raise a smile.
His monkey face will never fit,
and every glance he gives is vile.
He shuts his trap to please awhile –
to all it seems senile decay.
He opens up – they hate his style.
His tree lacks plums they always say.

49.

Like those poor crones who are so old
without a penny to call their own
when they see nubile girls of gold
nudging them off their pitch, they moan
to God and ask why they alone
were born before their time. Our Lord's
silent: he'd lose against a crone
like that in any war of words.

50.

THE OLD WOMAN REGRETS THE DAYS OF HER YOUTH

I heard the Lovely Armouress, [17]
as she was once so widely known,
complain in longing more or less
like this for youth again:
'You crone,
cat-thief and proud of it, you've thrown
me down and beaten me. But why?
Who cares if I split this bag of bones
and with the blow lie down and die?

51.

'You've knocked me off the high horse
my beauty rode over merchants, clerks
and priests. In those days, of course,
a passing shadow of the darks
that I could light and the bright sparks
would give their one and all, and leave
remorse till later after the larks.
Nothing a beggar now would thieve.

52.

'Yet I refused with most the men
(which wasn't very bright of me)
because I loved a fly boy then
and gave him all I had for free,

though sometimes going on the spree.
But, oh my Christ, I loved him well;
yet fast and loose he played with me
and only loved what I could sell.

53.

'He could have dragged me through Shit Street,
trodden me underfoot, and still
I would have loved him. He could beat
me up and break my back at will,
I'd soon forgive him all the ill
if once he asked me for a kiss.
The greasy glutton took his fill:
shame and despair have come from this.

54.

'But now he's dead these thirty years
while I survive grey-haired and old.
Oh, when I see what filth appears
when I am naked, I grow cold:
poor, dry, shrivelled, fold on fold.
What once I was, what now in age:
meagre and rank, nothing to hold –
I almost lose my mind in rage.

55.

'And where now has my smooth brow gone?
The arching eyebrows, the blonde hair?

The doe-like eyes whose glance could con
the canniest of men? And where
the fine proportioned nose; the pair
of intricate little ears; the chin
and dimple? My oval face so fair
with lovely lips and clearest skin?

56.

'Long arms; the deft fingertips?
The lovely small-boned shoulders; neat
breasts and the full rondure of hips,
smooth and compact enough to seat
the tourneyings when lovers meet?
Where the broad loins and pursing cunt
centred in plump firm thighs, discreet
with a little garden out the front?

57.

'My forehead's wrinkled, my hair grey,
my eyebrows thin, and sight grown dim
whose eyes once glanced and led my way
so many men. My ears once trim
hang down like moss, my face is grim,
colourless, dead, with furrowed chin,
nose far from beauty bent, a rim
of lips, fleshless as trod grapeskin.

58.

'So this is human beauty's end:
arms writhed, crazed hands too weak to lift,
back hunched until the shoulders bend.
My breasts? No tits to nudge a shift;
my tail the same, skin all adrift.
My quim, for Christ's sake! And thighs?
No more than hafts, skin, bone and rift,
all blotched like sausages.[18] Some prize!

59.

'That's how we regret the good times
among ourselves, peevish old fools,
squatting on our haunches in grime,
in grey heaps like balls of wool
around a hemp-stalk fire that cools.
The sooner flame, the sooner fall
of ash. We once were beautiful.
That's how it goes with one and all.'

60.

BALLADE.

So think it over, pretty Glover,[19]
my understudy once, and you,
Blanche, the Cobbler, take a lover.
Don't fuss for any man will do.
Think of yourselves before you're through.

Take right and left and down the line,
or like dud coins tucked in new
you'll have no currency or shine.

And you, sweet, keeping under cover
the spicy meat, the dance you do
entrances most; and you're another,
Jill, so good on carpets, too:
don't take your master in for you
will have to shut up shop in time
and take on some old priest to screw;
you'll have no currency or shine.

Hat-trick Jean, don't let your lover
set his cap elsewhere. And you,
Kate Purseproud, you will surely suffer
cock-teasing men with just the view.
Plain Jane gives a smile or two
but lovely sourpuss must decline.
In hideous age, with lovers few,
you'll have no currency or shine.

Girls for your own sake take my view.
Listen and learn how much I whine.
I cannot circulate; I'm through:
I have no currency or shine.

61.

This lesson was given them to learn
by one once fine and beautiful.
Rightly or wrong, you may discern.

I've made Fremin[20] (whose brain's a bull
in a chinashop) give it in full.
I'm sound in mind as ever I'll be.
I'll curse him if he tries to pull
your leg. Clerks show the mastery!

62.

The man in love must face in this
a great danger, that's clear to see.
To some these words will come amiss.
They'll tell me: 'Listen here to me.
If love has given you a flea
in the ear, you're the one to blame.
Your fear is crass stupidity
for these were women on the game.

63.

'If they just love to lay cash down
you only love them for your time.
They love at large men about town;
they laugh when purses weep, and climb
in bed with anything that's prime.
Women there are of faith and honour
where a decent man should pass his time
(so help me God!) or he's a goner.'

64.

It makes me sad to hear this said,
and to imagine talk like that.

For he concludes upon this head
(I see what he is driving at.)
that one should love and hang one's hat
in spots of virtue. But I suggest
the girls I stop to have a chat
were once as honest as the rest.

65.

Yes, and really honest, I mean,
without a spot of blame, though true
that when they came upon the scene
each took before they reached the stew,
a cleric, one; a layman, two;
a third some monk and served their turn
to quell the fires of love that grew
fiercer than St Antony's can burn.

66.

It's clear their lovers all obeyed
the words of the decree: they lay
in secret – love no others made.
But soon their love was given away
for she who has one part to play
gets bored with it and soon has done.
From then she much prefers to stray
and make a play for everyone.

67.

What drives them to it? I suppose,
without maligning woman's honour,
that from her nature clearly shows
the wish to have all men upon her.
I cannot rhyme the rest I ponder.
At Rheims or Troyes they all agree –
in Lille, St Omer, where you wander –
six navvies do more work than three.

68.

So foolish lovers take a knock,
their women take a broadside volley.
The only law in lovers' stock:
all faithfulness is merely folly,
however good the kiss, the dolly.
'In hawks and hounds, in love and war,'
everyone says the melancholy:
'one joy per hundred pains or more.'

69.

DOUBLE BALLADE[21]

So take your fill of love and go
to banquets, feasts and festivals.
You'll have so little left to show.
The only thing you'll bang's your skulls.
Love calls the beast out where it stalls.

Solomon turned to idols in the fit.
and Samson lost sight of his balls:
Happy the man who has none of it.

Orpheus, gentle minstrel, though,
playing his flutes in dying falls,
for love came face to face below
with four-headed Cerberus who snarls;
Narcissus, honest fellow, spoils
himself and drowns to kiss the spit
image of all his loving girls:
happy the man who has none of it.

Sardana, the knight to overthrow
the realm of Crete, liked yarns and balls
and wished to spin with girls and sew.
David, the King and prophet, lulls
his fear of God for it and falls
for bathing thighs compact and fit –
the woman washing in the pools:
happy the man who has none of it.

Ammon it gave the wish to know
(pretending tart the point of calls)
his sister Tamar. He laid her low
which was incestuous and false.
No joke either when Herod feels
St John's head quits his favourite
for dancing jig and snatch in veils:
happy the man who has none of it.

Of me, poor me, you now must know.
How I was thrashed like laundry, balls
naked. I see no need just now

to keep it dark. Catherine de Vauselles
it was that made me bear such brawls.
For Noel there, a similar hit
upon the night his wedding falls:
happy the man who has none of it.[22]

You'd think the randy fellow, though
would leave the easy lays and dolls?
Not even if burnt like men that go
upon a broomstick. Sweetness he smells
subtler than civet. Whatever falls
a man is mad to trust a bit,
blonde or brunette; they make us fools.
Happy the man who has none of it.

70.

If she whom once I used to serve
freely and faithfully – who brought
me so much torment, broke my nerve
and tortured me – had only thought
to say she merely wanted sport
when first we met (no mention, none!)
I might have ducked the net she caught
me with and had a little fun.

71.

No matter what I wanted to say
she always seemed quite keen to hear
without agreeing or giving way.
She'd even let me draw so near

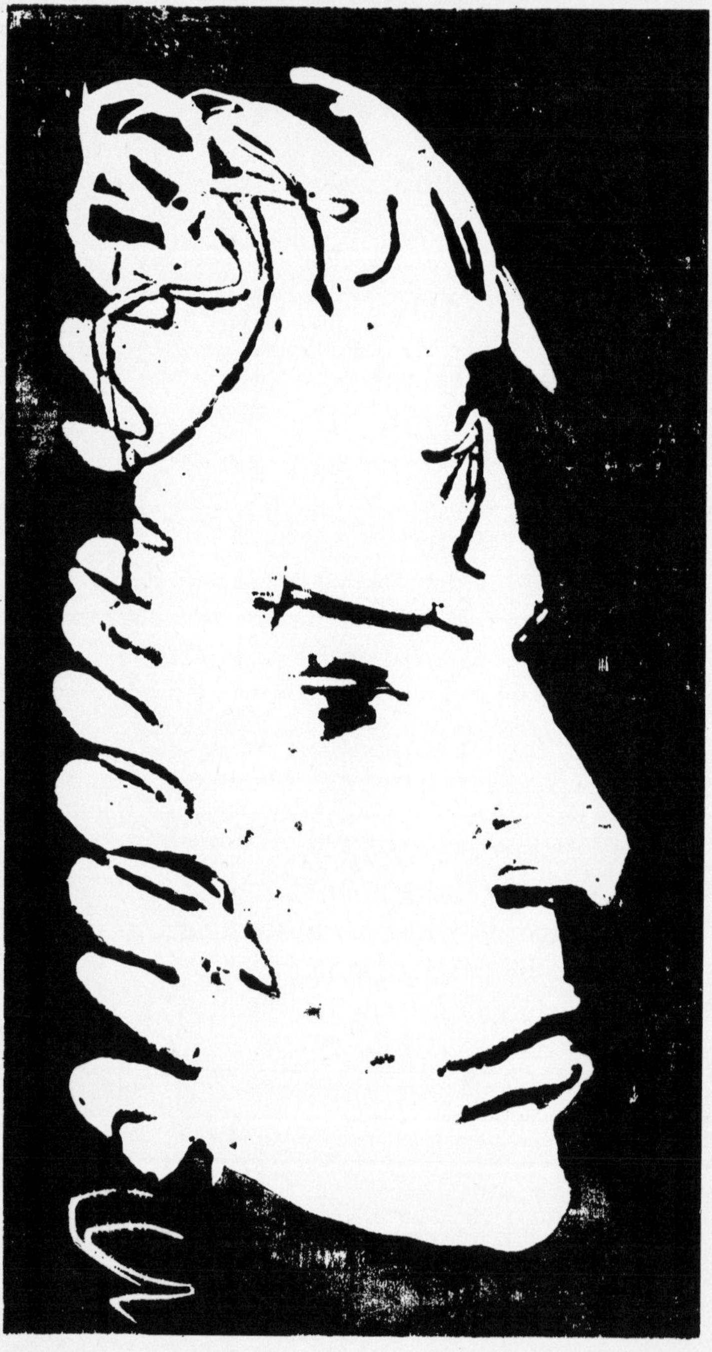

we touched as I whispered in her ear.
But she kept stringing me along
and let me make my love quite clear
only to laugh and do me wrong.

72.

Fooled me she did good and proper
that everything was otherwise:
flour was ash and clinker copper
and judge's hats were felt. Her dice
made snake's eyes double trey. Her eyes
said butter wouldn't melt in her mouth.
Liars accept each other's lies:
the moon is cheese and north is south,

73.

the sky a copper frying-pan,
and calfskin clouds water the crops;
and dusk was dawn when it began
and cabbage stumps were turnip tops,
and wine's best made from rotten hops;
a windmill is a war-machine
a skein of yarn the noose that drops,
a portly priest, a soldier lean.

74.

So love has made a fool of me
and run me out and locked the door.

No man has tricks enough, I see,
though mercurial his wits and more,
to come off lightly on this score
with even a rag to call his own.
Like me, he's beaten to the floor –
'The Reject Lover', I'm well-known.

75.

Hereby all loves I do renounce
and curse, defy with blood and fire.
My death by them comes at a pounce,
and none of them thinks to enquire.
I've no time now to ease desire;
my fiddle's down behind the bench.
If ever in those ranks or higher,
I swear that I no longer wench.

76.

I've pressed my finger to the leak;
follow me if you like the spray.
I'll leave this topic now and speak
of what I started out to say.
If any ask me why the way
I speak of love is so unkind,
then let this saying win the day:
'A dying man may speak his mind.'

77.

I feel the approaching of my thirst.
The gobs I hawk are cotton-white
and big as tennis balls that burst.
What more is there to say or write?
That Jill no longer likes the sight
of me, a broken-down old hack.
My voice is old and hoarse all right
but I'm still young and have the knack.

78.

Thank God – and Tacque Thibaud[23] as well
who pumped me full of water neat,
quartered me underground in hell
and not above, who chained my feet
and gave me chokepears free to eat –[24]
I'll pray for him, *et reliqua*;
may God grant him, oh yes, complete,
what I've in mind, *et cetera*.

79.

And yet I bear him no ill-will,
nor his lieutenant,[25] and none;
not even his official, still
a pleasant, accommodating one.
Yet with the rest I swear I've done,
except for little master Rob.
I love them, every mother's son,
as God loves Lombards at their job.

80.

Praise God that I remember well
certain bequests formerly framed
on my departure for a spell
in fifty-six. They have been named
The Testament by those who claimed
the pleasure which was never mine.
So what? It's commonly proclaimed:
'No man is master of his line.'

81.

I don't mean to revoke all these,
though there my lands are all at stake.
Nor could my pity ever freeze
for Bastard of the Bar. I make
a gift of my old mats to shake
down with the strawbales on his floors.
He'll get to grips on those and take
a firmer stand upon all fours.

82.

If any legacies I left
have gone astray, I order now
that on my death the few bereft
should find my heirs and make a row.
In case you ask me who or how:
Moreau, Provins, Turgis,[26] I said,
and tell them straight: all mine, I vow,
is theirs down to this very bed.

83.

In sum, I'll say just one more word
about it, then I must begin
my will. But first I want this heard
(my clerk Fremin will listen in
if he's not dozing off): herein
none shall be cut out of this will –
though I'd prefer no public din,
except in France a passing thrill.

84.

I feel my heart is growing weak
and I can hardly say a thing.
Fremin, sit by my bed; I speak
so people cannot pry; and bring
pen, paper, ink. My murmuring
take down in haste, have copies sent
out everywhere. I'm opening
my last will and testament:

85.

In the name of Eternal Father God,
and of his Son the Virgin bore
(Father eternal in our God),
and of the Holy Ghost who more
than saved all Adam lost before
and sends the damned to Heaven instead.
—You swallow that, your merit's poor:
bodies that turn to saints when dead!

86.

Dead were they all, body and soul,
and damned to doom for ever more:
souls to the flames; to dust the whole
body, no matter what before.
I make exception on this score
for prophet and for patriarch,
who, as I see it, never bore
the pain of arse on heat and stark.

87.

Though some will say, without a doubt,
'How dare you make remarks like these,
no theologian, you; it's out
and out presumption.'
A moment, please.
Jesus first made my point; he sees
Dives in Hell on no soft bed
while Lazarus who had no ease
has mounted high above his head.

88.

If Lazarus' finger had been hot
Dives would not have asked to feel
its coolness, nor to taste the spot
of water at its tip to heal
his burning throat. Guzzlers who peel
off coat and shirt for booze when broke
would not do well down there for real.
God save us all – and that's no joke.

89.

Now, in God's name, as I've just said,
and of his Glorious Mother, I pray
to finish off the work ahead
without more sin from me. I may
be ghostly thin and yet I say
cholera missed me by God's grace.
My other ills must now give way;
it's time to start in any case:

90.

First, my poor soul I now restore
to the blessed Trinity, consign
it to our Lady who once bore
our Lord, and pray that Heaven's Nine
Worthy Orders may incline
themselves in all their charity
and make this presentation of mine
before the precious throne for me.

91.

Item: I bequeath and leave my flesh
and bones to our great mother, earth.
The worms won't find it full or fresh
for hunger pinched its pennyworth.
Dispose it soon in its last berth.
From earth it yearned, to earth must yield.
Things always find their place on earth
if they don't wander far afield.

92.

Item: to Guillaume Villon, more
than father to me, gentler far
than mother with her child; a score
of scrapes he's got me out of – bar
this last that gave him quite a jar –
I beg him on my knees to let
me well alone to make or mar
this mess for all the joy I'll get.

93.

I leave my library for a start
to him – especially that work,
The Romance of the Devil's Fart,[27]
that Guy Tabary, an honest burke,
copied in notebooks which now lurk
beneath the table. A windy tale,
and yet the theme's enough to perk
the interest up should style fail.

94.

Item: I bequeath my poor mother
a prayer to Mary, Mother of God.
So much, God knows, I made her suffer
and rode all over her rough-shod.
When troubles pursue and I plod,
I have no other houseroom here
where I may rest my soul and body,
nor has my mother, the poor dear.

95.

BALLADE.

Lady of Heaven, Regent of Earth,
Empress of the Marshes of Hell,
welcome a christian of little worth
among your chosen ones to dwell
although my merits don't compel.
My Lady and my Mistress, your grace
is greater than my sin. No face
shall look on Heaven – this is no lie –
unless your goodness cover their case.
In this faith I mean to live and die.

So tell your son that by his birth
and death, I'm his. May he dispel
my sin and pardon me on earth
like Mary of Egypt, or as they tell,
Theophilus[28] who chose to sell
his soul to Satan for his place
and was acquitted by your grace.
Virgin who bore the Mass on High
save me from anything so base.
In this faith I mean to live and die.

A poor woman of little worth,
I'm ignorant, can't read or spell.
I see in church the heavenly mirth
of lutes and harps or the damned in Hell
boiling. One picture makes me well;
the second one I cannot face.
Give me that joy, Goddess of Grace

on whom all sinners at last rely
in no sham faith nor idle ways.
In this faith I mean to live and die.

Virgin, Princess, you bore, by grace
In you, Our Lord who reigns – though base,
Low he became and left his place,
Lord of All Power in Heaven on High,
Offering his youth to save our race.
Now is he Lord; I grant his case:
in this faith I mean to live and die.

96.

Item: to my dearest Rose[29]
neither my heart nor lights I give.
She'd jump at something else, God knows!
although she makes enough to live.
How? With a purse acquisitive,
silken and full and deep and wide.
But hang me or the next to give
a head or tail to toss inside.

97.

Even without me she gets enough;
such ploys no longer make me boil.
I'm finished with the sorry stuff.
I will not stand for further toil.
I cede my rights in her as spoil
to Michaux the Fearless Fucker's heirs.
Pray for him; take a jump right royal;
he lies at Saint Satur below Sancerre.

98.

And yet to square myself with love
rather than her – (she never dropped
a hint, a handkerchief or glove.
I don't know if all men have copped
the cold shoulder, and haven't stopped
wondering about it yet you see,
but by St Mary's beauty, I opt
for one great belly laugh from me) –

99.

I send her this ballade in 'O'.
Who'll give it her? Now let me see.
Why Perrenet of the Bar will go
only providing he'll agree
if he should meet while roaming free
my lady whose nose is out of joint
he'll say without ado for me:
'You slut, which way do you point?'

100.

BALLADE: TO HIS GIRL-FRIEND.

Fake beauty whose cost to me is real;
Rough were the facts, all sweetness was the show;
A love tougher on the teeth than steel,
Named now there's little more to undergo.
Charming your stealth that dealt my heart the blow;
One pride, your secret, was to cut men dead.
Your eyes are pitiless; won't Justice show
Some cure for man – no knock upon the head.

More worth my while it were to make appeal
Anywhere else, and honour keep; but no,
Really there's nothing lures me from her heel.
Take off I must with only shame to show.
Help me, help me, anyone, high or low!
Eh what? Or shall I die before I shed
a blow? Won't pity hear my cry and show
some cure for man – no knock upon the head.[30]

Toward your flower, blooming now, will steal
a time to wither, dry and fade the glow.
I'll laugh then if my jaws can make a meal
of it. But no; it would be madness – no!
Old then myself and you but an old crow.
So drink deep while freshets fill the bed.
Don't mark them all with tortures I can show:
some cure for man – no knock upon the head.

Prince of love whom lovers serve below,
don't shift your favour from me for what's said:
frank hearts should for our Saviour show
some cure for man – no knock upon the head.

101.

Item: to Ythier Marchant[31] to whom
I left my sword not long before
I now bequeath ten lines of gloom
to which he must prepare a score

for lute and voice to mourn the more
his former girls: a *De Profundis*.
Their proper name I shall ignore
or he'd hate me for a month of Sundays.

102.

Death, I appeal against your rigour.
My mistress you abduct and rape,
and from your urge none can escape:
you have embraced my nerveless figure.

Since then I've lost all sense of vigour.
In life, she left you in good shape.
Death, I appeal against your rigour,
my mistress you abduct and rape.

Though two, we lived in nothing bigger
than the heart: I can't escape
if hers is dead; I'll die or scrape
through as a likeness, a carved figure.

103.

Item: for master Jean Cornu[32]
I'd like to leave one more bequest
for he has always helped me through
in times of need and bitter test.
I give him then with all the rest
Bobignon's garden, rented me

provided I had the gable dressed
and fixed the door on tenancy.

104.

Because that door was gone I lost
a hoe-shaft there and paving-stone.
Not eight, not even ten hawks tossed
inside could ever catch a lone
lark. Though if the bolt is thrown
the house is safe. I slung my hook
there as my sign but that has flown.
A hard and bloody night to the crook!

105.

Item: and though the wife of master
Pierre St Amant[33] (if she's to blame
may God forgive her my disaster)
made me a beggar – all the same,
to *The White Horse* who's never game,
in part-exchange I give a mare;
and to *The She-Mule*, hardly tame,
a red-hot ass that's going spare.

106.

Item: fourteen barrels of wine,
taken from Turgis, that I select
at my own risk, I would assign
Sire Dennis Hesselin,[34] Elect
of Paris. If he drinks unchecked

until his reason floods and drowns,
top up with water. For wine has wrecked
many fine houses in the towns.

107.

Item: I give my lawyer my sword –
Guillaume Charruau – although
I left it last to Marchant. (No word
about the sheath!) A fartthing or so
he'll get in change and that will go
to bloat his purse, found in the square
or flag-stoned walks around the show-
place of the Templars – somewhere there!

108.

Item: to Fournier,[35] my advocate,
for all the thankless tasks he's done
(this time my costs are moderate),
for all the cases he has won,
and justly, by God's only Son!
– four fistfuls of my purse, all-told.
Justice was done. Good cause there's none
unless the lawyer's good as gold.

109.

Item: I leave *The Great Wine Cup*,
Place de Grève, to Master Jacques
Raguier[36] as long as he'll pay up
four plackets – though, to get his whack

he'll have to sell what hides the slack
from thigh to calf, and go bare-skin
in pumps, if he won't take his tack
and drink with me in *The Pine Cone Inn.*

110.

As for Merbeuf and Louviers,[37]
I leave them neither bull nor cow
for they're no stockmen. More truly they
are men to carry hawks (now, now,
don't think this is a joke!) to bow
and stoop on partridges and plover,
without a failure anyhow –
at Madam Machecoue's and under cover.

111.

Item: should Turgis come to me
I'll pay the draught drawn on his cellar.
To find my place he'll need to be
much sharper than a fortune-teller.
Parisian-born and city-dweller,
I'll give him my right of magistrate,
for if I sound a southern fellow
two women taught my tongue the trait.

112.

And both now live at St Generoux,
a charming and a pretty pair,

on the borders of Brittany-Poitou,
near St Julien de Vouvantes there.
But nobody is larnin' wheare
somever these ladies pass the day.
I baint so daaft I do decleare:
I like to 'ide my luves away.[38]

113.

I give to Jean Raguier,
the sergeant of the Twelve, so long
as he shall live, a cheese soufflé,[39]
daily from Bailly's, good and strong,
to stuff his gob, then go along
to wet his whistle at the côte
de Maubué. Eating, right or wrong,
has never bested him, I note.

114.

Item: I give the Prince of Fools,
Michault de Four[40] to make a pair;
he sometimes cracks a good one, drools
'My Sweetest Love' with quite a flair.
I give him good day and do declare
if he brushed things up a little bit,
he's fairly foolish when he's there,
and when he's not all there, a wit.

115.

Item: of the Two Hundred and Twenty
Sergeants,[41] because their work's so straight,

and since they are so good and gentle,
to Dennis Richier, Vallette, his mate:
a velvet chinstrap to take the weight
right off the feet. I mean, of course,
the ones on foot, for to this date,
I haven't dealt with those on horse.

116.

I give to Perrenet,[42] once more,
the Bastard of the Bar, I mean,
– a cleancut fellow at the core –
to change the bar sinister seen
upon his arms, a markedly clean
new deck of cards; three loaded dice;
what else? And if he farts out lean
or loud, the quartern fever, twice!

117.

Item: I wish Cholet[43] would stop
dovetailing, butting and pegging board,
his hooping jugs and kegs, and swap
his tools for a good Lyons sword.
His cooper's mallet he may hoard.
However much he'd like to quit
joinery of his own accord,
he likes to knock and bang a bit.

118.

Item: to John the Wolf I give
(a splendid man in part-exchange!)
since he's too frail and thin to live,
and Cholet's hunting is so strange,
a fine little setter with the range
to keep the birds from taking wing.
To cover up I will arrange
for tabards cloaking everything.

119.

Item: the Woodsmith[44] I will stock
with Moslem ginger, a hundred bits
with heads and tails; but not to lock
in box or jar, but ass-over-tits
to sew up eels and thighs of chits
and bloat the belly out so much
that nipples stand with milk, and fits
of blood descend to balls and crutch.

120.

Item: to Captain Riou,[45] the same
as for his archers, I bequeath
the meat of six wolves' heads that came
from butchers' dogs, then left to seethe
in cooking wine, not fit to teeth
a swineherd on. To taste such prime
meat once, almost all men that breathe
would readily indulge in crime.

121.

Though heavier, this kind of meat,
than feathers, cork or down, it's fit
for soldiers in the field to eat
and during siege it helps a bit.
If wolves were trapped, and dogs that split
the hunt, they'd make fur-linings in
his winter coat. I order it
as doctor just to save his skin.

122.

Item: Robinet Trascaille[46] who rides
to work on a fat and hefty horse
(and mounts it well) but never strides
as would a quail – on him, I force
a dish he is too shy, of course,
to borrow from my little hob.
His household's made with this resource
and nothing's lacking for the job.

123.

Item: I give Perrot Girart,
sworn barber of Bourg la Reine,
two bowls and a big-bellied jar
since he slaves to make ends meet again.
Six years ago it must be when
he forcefed me a week on fat
porkers in his private den.
The Abbess of Pourras[47] swears to that!

124.

Item: to the Mendicant Brothers,
Daughters of God and the Beguines
of Paris and Orleans, the others,
those male and female Turlupines,
I'll make oblation by all means
of good thick Jacobin soup and custard.
Then pros and cons behind the scenes
for contemplation may be mustered.

125.

Don't look at me. I give them less
than any mother and mother's son,
or God who so awards success
on those who suffer for their fun.
These fine fathers, like everyone,
must live – and those of Paris, too.
They give our women a pleasant run
and prove their love to husbands true.

126.

Though Jean de Poullieu had his say
on this, they forced him to retract
in public. Jean de Meung made play
of all their ploys when he attacked
as did Matheolus in his tract.
But we must honour and obey
everything and anything in fact
that's honoured by the Church today.

127.

So I, their servant, shall submit
myself in all I do or say
to honour them as they see fit
with open heart, and to obey
without back-chat in any way.
It's mad exposing their affairs
and better not to have your say.
Public or private, vengeance is theirs.

128.

Item: to brother Baude who lives
among the Carmelites, so brash
and big he acts, I'd like to give
a helmet and two pikes to bash
de Tusca and his men if rash
enough to rob his bird's rib-cage.[48]
He's old; if his sword still cuts a dash
he is the devil of an age.

129.

And since the Keeper of the Seal
has so much beedung now to chew
and is so worthy, let me deal
him out pre-spittled wax, a screw
to crush his thumb to help him do
imprint and sealing in one go.
The Bishop's Clerk shall have his due
and God treat all the others so.

130.

As for my lords the auditors,
I'll panel out their barns; on those
that suffer in the arse with sores
some seatless chairs I would dispose.
For Little Macée, one of the pro's
of Orleans who took my money belt,
a hefty fine may they impose.
The awful shit, she always smelt.

131.

Item: for swearing by St George
and God when dubbed a knight, I'll fix
up de la Vacquarie with a gorget[49]
of simple Scottish make – for kicks,
since all who saw and heard his tricks
could never speak or think of it
without bursting out like lunatics
and laughing till their sides would split.

132.

Because he has his parents' sin
of drinking kilderkin and cask,
I leave Jean Laurens now the thin
linings of my bags, and ask
that every morning he makes his task
to wipe his poor red eyes quite clear.
Archbishops of Bourges may use a mask
of silk – but that is very dear.

133.

Item: to master Jean Cotart,
my lawyer in the Church's Court,
(I owe him just a penny so far
I think, or something not far short
from when Denise once had me brought
before the law because, she said,
I had abused her) this prayer I've wrought
to rest his soul now he is dead:

134.

BALLADE AND PRAYER

Our father Noah who planted the vine,
and you too, Lot, who drank in a cave
till love that makes men foolish swine
had you and your daughters misbehave
(I don't reproach you though it's grave!)
Architriclinus – a master you are –
I plead with all of you to save
the soul of my late Jean Cotart.

For he descended from your line:
the best he drank, could never save
a penny to spend. A mighty fine
guzzler he was; he'd never waive
his round; he laboured like a slave
and none could drag him from his jar.
Lords, do not bar his way but save
the soul of my late Jean Cotart.

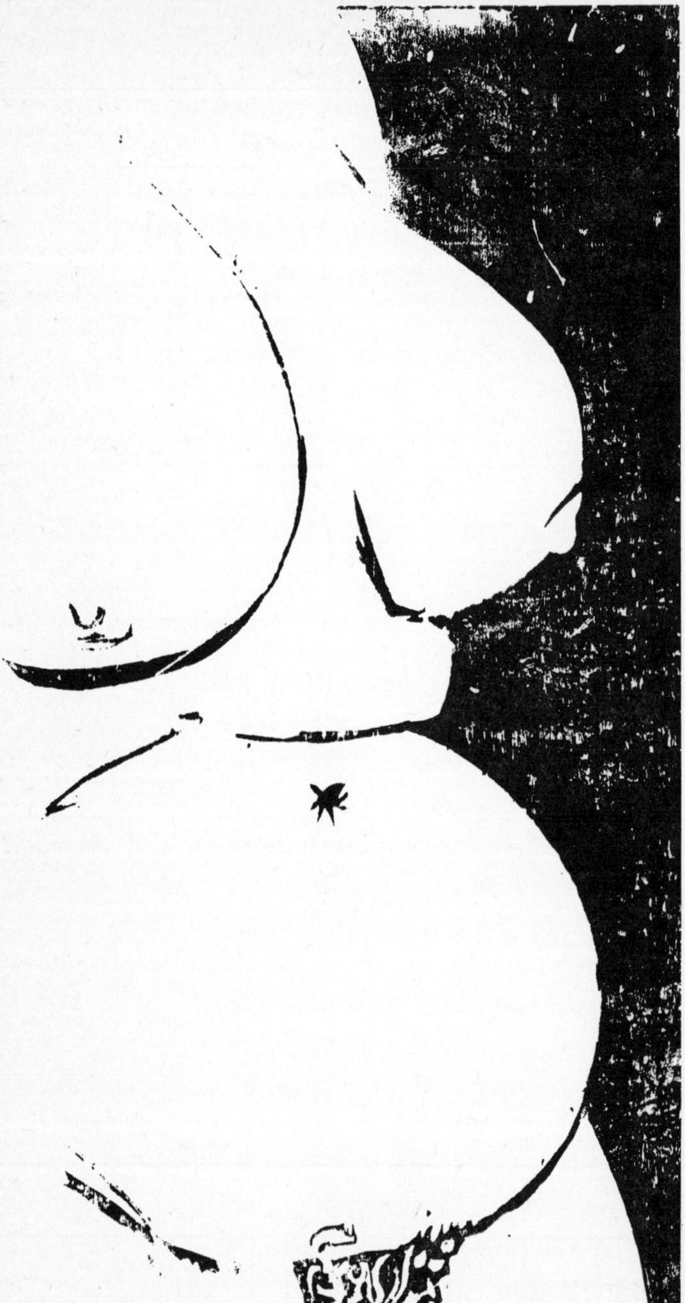

A drunk, he'd reel and roll in wine.
Some nights I used to see him waver
home. One memory of mine,
the butcher's stall and the close shave
he had. No other drunkard gave
me such delight in any bar.
Open the gates; you hear him rave –
the soul of my late Jean Cotart.

Prince, his spit wouldn't reach the paving.
He used to roar: 'My throat will char.'
A thirst that never quenched its craving:
the soul of my late Jean Cotart.

135.

Item: I'd like young Merle to take
in hand my money-changing rôle.[50]
(I do it against my will) but make
this stipulation for the whole:
to friend and stranger he must dole
out two heads to a single tail
(though cracked within the ring they roll).
Lovers should live on liberal scale.

136.

Item: while travelling, I found
my three poor orphans fully grown,
no muttonheads but fairly sound.
From here to Salins, no kids known

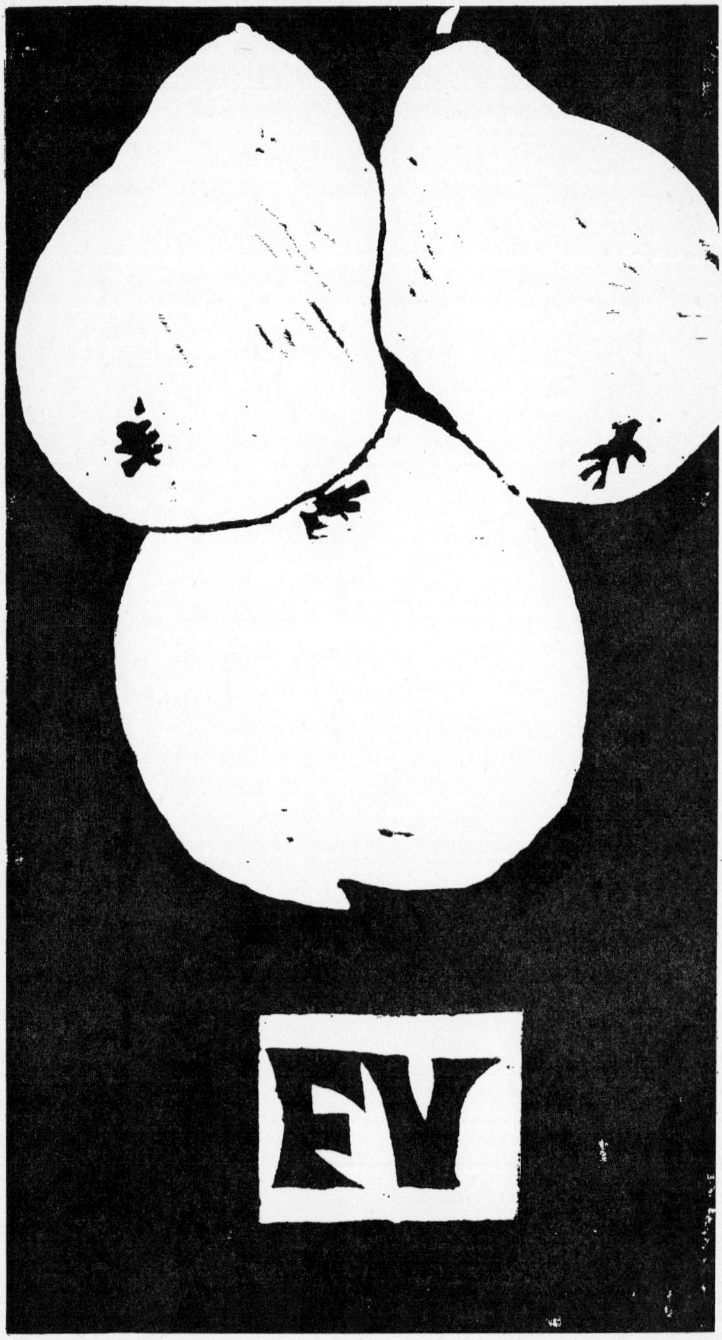
FV

have learnt so well the lessons shown
and salted them away. I swear
by the order of Bedlamites, youth flown
like that is not a fool's affair.

137.

And now I'd like them finished off.
But where? Richier's not too hard;
the *Donatus* they'll never cough
up with. But nothing must retard
them, so they ought to make their yard:
Ave salus, tibi d'écus[51] – then stop!
All further study they must discard.
Scholars don't always reach the top.

138.

They'll learn as much as this, then wo!
I must insist they end their stint.
Such innocents could never show
the great Credo[52] a single glint
of interest. I'll pay – by dint
of selling half my tabard split
in two – and stand them each a mint.
All youngsters like to have a bit.

139.

Manners they must be taught although
a thrashing is the only way.

Their hoods must fit, their thumbs must go
into their belts and they must say
humbly to all they meet each day:
'Hm, what? Oh no, that's quite all right.'
Then some will say and well they may:
'Now that's what I would call polite.'

140.

Item: to those poor little clerks
I signed my titles to of late,
as straight as ramrods and bright sparks,
one look has dispossessed my state
and I renounce for them the wait
(as good as theirs in any case
consigned in court on such a date)
for rent on Guillaume Gueldry's place.

141.

Although they're young and harum-scarum,
they don't upset me – boys will be boys.
Thirty-odd years if God will spare them
and they'll grow out of tricks and toys.
It's wrong to cut up rough, annoys
with children well-behaved and good.
The birch is what a fool employs;
children turn people as they should.

142.

The Eighteen Clerks will pay their keep
with their own pensions. I'll work that out
myself for them since they won't sleep
like dormice hibernating. No doubt
how sorry is that sleeping bout
where youth finds ease in youth. It takes
such hold on them they do without
when old they need to rest their aches.

143.

And letters similar to these
I'll send the collator. Let them pray
for me, their benefactor, please.
But someone clip their ears if they
refuse. Some people think the way
I care for these is strange. I'll swear
at feast nor fast I never lay
an eye upon their mothers there.

144.

Item: I give to Michault Culdoe,
and Sire Charlot Taranne as well,
a hundred sous. If they must know
how come, they needn't fret; it fell
like manna. And should they do as I tell,
a pair of sheepskin boots[53] with uppers
and soles: Jeanne and another belle
they'll have to take and groom their cruppers.

145.

Item: I leave to Grigny's Lord
to whom I gave Bicêtre before,
the Billy Tower to be restored
where there's a window or a door
unfit to function any more.
He can afford to have it done.
To left and right let money pour.
I need the cash and he has none.

146.

Item: to Thibaud of the Guard
(Thibaud? That's cuckoo! Jean's the name)[54]
what shall I give that won't come hard?
Too thick and fast my losses came
this year. May God restore the same.
Amen! Good Lord, *The Keg of Wine*,
of course. Though Genevois has more claim
with his great age and nose for sign.

147.

A basket full of cloves I leave
Basanier, the notary
and criminal clerk, that he may thieve
from Jean de Ruel, and equally
to Mautaint and Rosnel to see
that with a lowly swift accord
they serve this gift of cloves from me
to St Christopher's devoted lord.

148.

I give him this ballade[55] to toast
his lady who has all the charms.
If love is not so fair to most,
no wonder, for by feat of arms
he won her in the lists' alarms,
that René King of Sicily held.
As Hector or Troilus won their palms
without a vaunt – so he excelled.

149.

BALLADE

At break of day the falcon claps his wings
More from pleasure and custom than for flight;
Blackbird sings and dances for joy which brings
Right to his feathers the mate who loves the sight.
Oh, then I burn within to take delight
In you and give you what would please all lovers.
So know how love writes this on sheets of white:
Enjoy the end we reach between the covers.

Dear to my heart beyond all reasonings,
Entirely mine till death consumes my light;
Laurel so sweet you still my sufferings;
Olive so frank you end my bitter fight.
Reason would rear me into your delight;
Even my will agrees to keep us lovers,
to serve you as my customary right,
enjoy the end we reach between the covers.

And what is more, in all my sufferings,
under a fortune often angry, the light
of your soft look destroys her menacings,
no more, no less than wind blows smoke from sight.
I do not sow the seed in soil that's light
but in your fields my oats and not another's.
God wills I fork and fertilize it right:
enjoy the end we reach between the covers.

Princess, listen to what I now recite:
my heart shall never turn from you to others.
I won't have it. Nor yours from mine take flight:
enjoy the end we reach between the covers.

150.

Item: to Sire Jean Perdrier, nix,
and to his younger brother Francis.
They always helped me in a fix
and shared their goods and took their chances
even although my partner Francis
half prayed, half ordered me to try
a dish in Bourges, one of his fancies:
raw tongue and searing hot and high!

151.

So out I went and took a look
in Taillevent, the chapter there
on fricassees. I read the book,
the length and breadth and depth with care
but found no mention of the fare;

still, here's Macquaire's great recipe
(he devilled Satan in his hair).
I swear to you he gave it me:

152.

BALLADE[56]

In arsenic and sulphurous and pure,
in orpiment, in quicklime and salt-petre.
in boiling lead (the way to kill or cure)
in pitch and soot soaking in lye and beaten
in turds and piss, the wash of leper's feet,
in toe-jam and the clods from soles of boots,
in viper's blood, poisonous drugs and shoots,
in bile of badgers, wolves and foxes, dried,
in frogspawn and the hash of squirming newts
may these envious tongues be fried and fried.

In brains of blackest cat that can't endure
to fish – so old it has no teeth to eat;
and in the drool and drivel which I'm sure
will do of some old mastiff now dead-beat,
mad and foaming at the mouth; then heat
in lather from a wheezing mule when the brute's
diced with good sharp scissors; next dilute
with water where the rats have ducked both hide
and snout, where lizards, snakes and reptiles root,
may these envious tongues be fried and fried.

In sublimate dangerous to touch; then skewer
and stuff into a living snake made sweet

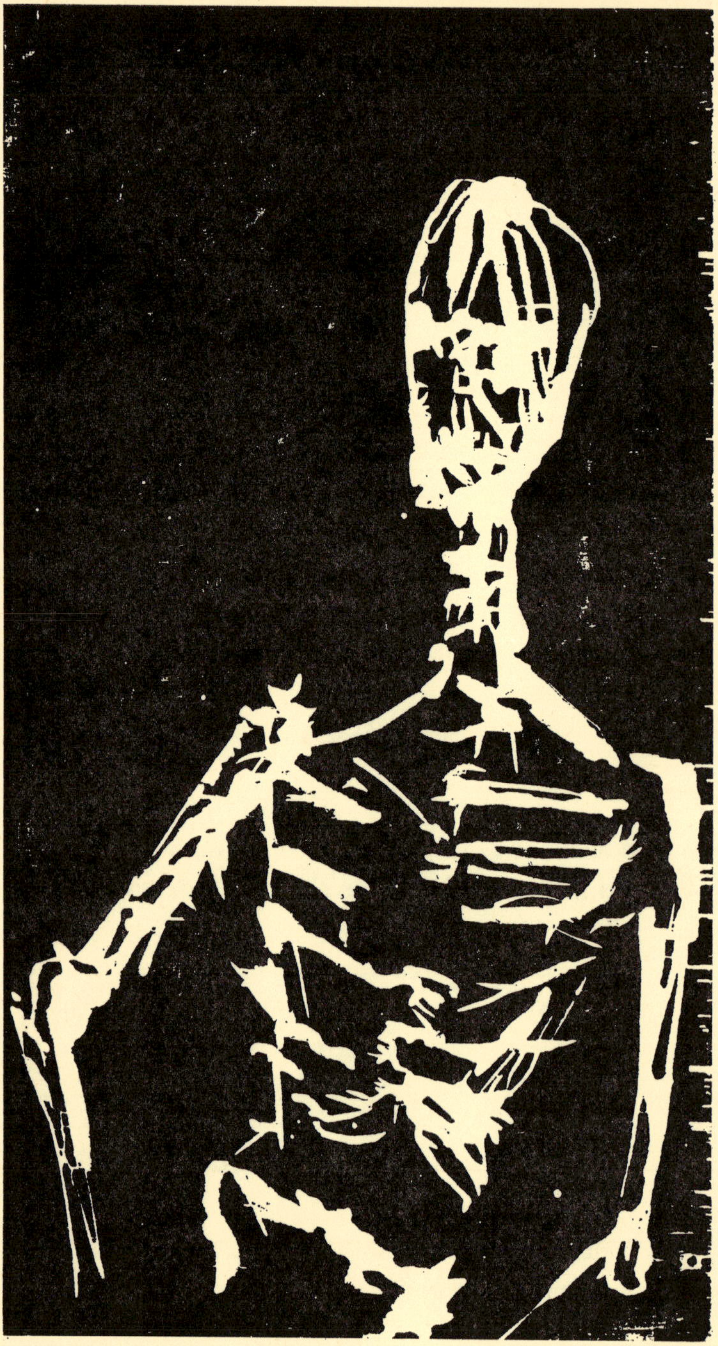

with blood dried in a barber's porringer,
like chives a blackish green, when the moon's complete,
in chancres and tumours cooked in bowls where sheets
and nappies soak for wet-nurses; or shoot
the lot in tubs used by the whoring beauties.
(If you are one who's never seen inside
a brothel you'll not guess the tub's true duties.)
May these envious tongues be fried and fried.

Prince, take all these tasty curried fruits
and if you lack a colander then shoot
the lot through dirty pants and wring till dried
but first in pigshit or any swinish brute's
may these envious tongues be fried and fried.

153.

Item: for Andry Courault alone
Franc Gontier[57] I will refute.
I ask the tyrant on his throne
for nothing. The poor should not dispute,
the Sage has said, nor press his suite
against the great. They lay the lines
and spread the nets and run the shoot
to catch him in their own designs.

154.

But Gontier I do not fear.
He has no men; he is the heir
to nothing more than me, so here
we are in argument, one where

he praises poverty as his share
to last the summer and winter long.
He sees all happiness right there
in pauperdom. Let's see who's wrong:

155.

BALLADE

A plump canon lolled on pillows of down
beside a stove in a room well carpeted,
and Dame Sidoine lay there without her gown,
white and smooth and soft, with stylish head.
On hippocras all day and night they fed.
They laughed and toyed around, kissed and caressed;
and flesh to flesh for greater ease they pressed.
– I saw them through the keyhole, learnt from these
that for alleviating sorrow best
no treasure's quite like living at your ease.

If Gontier and Helen had got down
to lead a life as sweet as this was led
they wouldn't give a toss for junkets, brown
soups, shallots and onions on which they fed
till the breath stank. A diet, I'd have said,
not worth a clove of garlic. Then they rest
beneath a rose and proud of it! What's best?
A bed and bedside chair? Which, if you please?
What need is there to make a further test?
No treasure's quite like living at your ease.

They live on oaten bread that's coarse and brown
and drink the stream from breakfast-time till bed.

All birds from here to Babylon, up or down,
could never make me stick water and bread
a single day – a morning, I should have said!
My God! Let Gontier and Helen nest
beneath the wild rose tree. If that seems best
it's up to them. And though one partly sees
the dignity of labour and the rest –
no treasure's quite like living at your ease.

Prince, settle the question I suggest;
but as for me (not wishing to displease)
when I was young I often heard expressed:
no treasure's quite like living at your ease.

156.

Item: because she knows her Bible,
my Lady of Bruyères,[58] I grant
her and her girls without a rival
the right to preach from any cant –
except the gospels – so their rant
may save whores sharp in tongue and voice.
Outside the graveyards, or it can't
be done; the Linen Market's choice.

157.

BALLADE

Although they have the slickest patter,
Venetian girls and Florentines,
the crones as well, come to the matter,

ready enough as go-betweens;
though Lombards, Romans spill the beans
and Genoese – I'll risk it then! –
from Piedmont to Savoyard scenes
there is no tongue like Parisienne.

In Naples they hold chairs in chatter
to teach them what the other means;
German and Prussian women natter;
and yet although they may be queans
of Egypt, Greece or Hungarian scenes
or fetch from other field or fen;
Spanish or Catalonian colleens,
there is no tongue like Parisienne.

Bretons and Swiss can only smatter
like Toulouse Jills and Gascon Jeans.
Fishwives of Petit Pond'd scatter
all the lot in making scenes –
and Calais girls and libertines
of England, (I've got around again!)
and Picard girls of Valence. It means
there is no tongue like Parisienne.

Prince, to Parisian colleens
award the gift of the gab again,
and never mind Italian queans:
there is no tongue like Parisienne.

158.

Look at them in twos or threes
sitting on hems of their long gear

in churches or in monasteries.
Don't put them off, but draw quite near;
such judgments you will overhear
as Macrobius never dared to make.
The barest facts they make quite clear;
you'd learn a lesson you could take.

159.

Item: to Montmartre Mount, a place
that is a very ancient monument,
I give, and lay upon its base,
Mount Valerian – and the unspent
quarter of pardon it's my intent
to bring from Rome – so many more
Christians will poke about and enter
an abbey no man has known before.

160.

The chambermaids and serving men
from wealthy households (and why not?)
make good tarts, strong cheesecake, then
they have a ball upon the dot
of midnight. Eight pints on the trot
will hardly warm them up, while lord
and lady sleep. I'll teach the lot
a quiet game of asses scored.

161.

Item: to wealthy girls who still
have fathers, mothers, aunts, by God,
I'll give them nothing in my will.
I've shot their servants such a wad.
They don't demand a lot: the odds
and ends would give a power of pleasure
to poor young maids that now a squad
of Jacobins pick about at leisure,

162.

Carthusians as well and Celestines,
who, even though the order's strict
usually dine beyond their means;
the girls get plates already licked.
Perrette and Jackie I have picked
and 'Christ-yes' Isabel to bear
witness to hungers they inflict.
Who's hellbound giving girls the fare?

163.

Item: to Fat Margot who's so fair
of face and painted, as I see,
devoted as she is, I swear
I love her for herself and she
loves me the way I've got to be.
If you come across the dear sweet soul
upon your travels make her free
with this ballade and read the whole:

164.

BALLADE

I love and serve my lady with a will,
but that's no reason you should call me mad.
For her, I'd hitch on sword and shield to kill.
She is the goods to please my every fad.
When customers arrive, I lightly pad
to bring in pots and wine. I serve them cheese
and fruit, and bread and water as they please
and say (depending on the tip I'm paid)
'Do call again and come here at your ease
in this whorehouse where we do a roaring trade.'

But then fine feelings end and turn to ill.
When she comes home without the cash, I'm had.
I cannot stand her, she has blood to spill.
I hate her, grab her belt, gown, shift and plaid
and swear I'll flog the lot and her to add
up for the loss of all the nightly fees.
But hands on hips she hollers if you please
how I am anti-Christ and won't get paid.
I grab a club and sign her, nose to knees,
in this whorehouse where we do a roaring trade.

We make peace then in bed. She takes my fill,
gorged like a dung-beetle, blows me a bad
and mighty poisonous fart. I fit her bill
she says, and laughing bangs my nob quite glad.
She thwacks my thigh and, after what we've had,
dead drunk we sleep like logs – and let the fleas.
Though when we stir her quim begins to tease.

She mounts; I groan beneath the weight – I'm splayed!
Her screwing soon will bring me to my knees
in this whorehouse where we do a roaring trade.

Vary the wind, come frost, I live in ease.
I am a fucker; she fucks as I please.
Layman or laity – no matter of degrees!
Layer on layer of onion overlaid,
Our filth we love and filths upon us seize;
Now we flee honour, honour from us flees
in this whorehouse where we do a roaring trade.

165.

Item: to the Idol Marion
and big Jean of Brittany
I give them leave to carry on
a school where all the mastery
is pupil power for a fee.
These studies go on everywhere
except the jail of Meung maybe.
To hell with signs; the trade's not rare.

166.

Item: to Noel Jolis I lash
out, giving him only a birch
fresh from my garden. Without cash
I leave him now right in the lurch.
Chastisement according to the Church
makes a good alms. He shouldn't mind.
I order Henry gives the urchin
two hundred and twenty strokes behind.

167.

Item: I don't know how to endow
the Hotel Dieu nor any poor
hospitals. No joking matter now,
it's not the place. The poor have more
than their fair share of ills in store.
Everyone's scraps are in their range.
Friars cooked my goose and left the poor
the bones. To little men small change.

168.

Item: to Colin Galerne, my barber,
next to the herbalist Angelot's,
I give a great ice-block to harbour
in his bosom. From? The floes
of Marne. To last the winter snows
hug it against the guts; and so,
if winter long he holds the pose
next summer's heat won't make him glow.

169.

Item: to Foundlings, sweet Fanny Adams.
The Lostlings need consoling more.
They turn up usually at Madam's,
at Marion the Idol's door.
A single lesson on this score
I'll read, and one that flies right past.
Blockheads they mustn't be, but pore
upon it since it is the last:

170.

Fair children take care not to lose
the rose's bloom beneath your hat.
You clerks with fingers like some glues,
if it's Montpipeau you're aiming at,
or Rueil, don't risk your neck for that.
For knocking off on either job
and making an appeal too pat
Colin de Cayeux[59] lost his nob.

171.

The game is hardly worth the candle:
body and sometimes soul it takes.
The loser dies in shame and scandal
no matter what repentance he makes.
And he who gets the lucky breaks
won't win the hand of Dido, Queen
of Carthage. The man's a fool who stakes
so great a prize to win a bean.

172.

Now listen all of you: they say
the profits on the draught are spent
upon the drayman on the way,
in woods in summer, in winter bent
over a fire. No cash is lent –
all given, so lash out all you owe;
don't leave behind a single cent
for easy come is easy go.

173.

BALLADE

Whether you counterfeit your brass
and end so oiled you boil and bake,
traitors whose credit wouldn't pass;
or peddle pardons; learn to shake
the loaded dice; or maybe take
to filching in and out of doors –
where does it go, the money you make?
All to the taverns and the whores.

Rhyme or rail or clash your brass,
like shameless fools that always fake;
mime, mum, or try some magic pass;
or if in towns and cities, make
miracles, mysteries, jigs; or take
a trick or two or skittle scores –
soon gained, soon gone! (You still awake?)
All to the taverns and the whores.

If depths like these are not your class,
then plough up fields or drive a rake;
or turn to doctoring horse and ass.
But only if you cannot take
to book and pen. A crust you'll make.
Yet if you've slaved at prison chores
you haven't lifted loot to take
all to the taverns and the whores.

Before you do much worse then, take
trousers and shoes and all that's yours,
gowns and the silks for your own sake
all to the taverns and the whores.

174.

It's you I'm talking to, old friends,
sick in the soul, in body sound:
keep out of wind and sun that sends
men black and blue. Don't hang around,
its bite is bitter, you may be bound.
So do your best to pass things by.
For God's sake, bear in mind the sound:
There is a time for you to die.

175.

Item: I give the Fifteen Score[60]
(Three Hundred the name should be)
not those of Paris, Provins, for
I feel they have some claim on me:
they'll have my glasses, I agree,
so they can clearly tell the face
of good from bad in the cemetery
des Innocents. But not the case!

176.

There is no play or laughter here.
What good was wealth to them, to lie
in great fourposters, and what cheer
their paunches big with wine, the high
days, feasts and balls, the standing by
for one more giddy whirl. They're gone,
all of the pleasures they could try;
the evil that they did lives on.

177.

I think of all the skulls that pile
inside the charnel houses here:
past masters of requests awhile
in the Treasury at least; or mere
porters instead; no longer clear
which one is which. I cannot say
this was a bishop; this would appear
a lantern-maker in his day.

178.

These heads have bowed and scraped to one
another once. Some ruled the roost,
some served in awe; all dead and done.
I see their bodies all reduced
pellmell to heaps, the lands they used
to run usurped. There is no leave
for any appeal to be produced.
Master or clerk, there's no reprieve.

179.

God rest their souls now they are dead.
As for their bodies, they are dust,
lords though they were and ladies fed
tenderly, sweetly on cream and custard,
pudding and rice. Their bones are just
fined down to powder; they have no call
for laughter, no jig for joy or lust.
May sweet Jesus absolve them all.

180.

For all those dead and gone I make
this legacy and make it plain
to regents, courts, tribunals that take
a stand against all greed, and drain
their bones and bodies to sustain
the common good. By God and by
St Dominic,[61] may they all gain
their absolution when they die.

181.

Item: for Jacques Cardon, nix.
I've nothing decent left for him
but I won't leave him in a fix.
Perhaps a song will take his whim.
The tune is 'Marionette' a hymn
to Marion the Skintight; or try
'Open your door, Guillemette', a trim
piece that might serve for mustard pie.

182.

SONG

On my return from the harsh prison
where I almost lost my life,
if Fate has even now her knife
in me, you judge of her decision:
it seems to me, without derision

she now should put an end to strife,
on my return.
If she is mad beyond revision
and I no longer may survive,
pray God my rapt soul may arrive
within his house above when risen,
on my return.

183.

Item: to Master Lomer I give,
since I was fairy born, the jinx
of love while he's unamative
from cover girl and hatless minx!
And may he plug a hundred chinks
a night that cost him a mere nut,
despite whatever Ogier thinks,
that great Dane with a nose for smut.

184.

Item: for couples who can't quite make it –
beside the Chartier[62] bequest –
an aspersorium of naked
tears, with a sprig of wild rose dressed,
beside their bed to beat their breast,
forever green to cast aspersion –
so long as they will sing to rest
poor Villon's soul with psalms in person.

185.

Item: to Jacques James I wish
(he'll kill himself to make a mint)
that he may pick and choose his dish
but marry no one. The skinflint
will claim to all but kin he's skint.
His sole concern is where to dine.
The filth of sows, to drop a hint,
most rightfully belongs to swine.

186.

The Seneschal with the snub nose
(who once from debt bought my release)
in recompense I now propose
to make a smith to shoe the geese
and ducks.[63] I send these jokes to please
him. Never mind if he desires
to make light with them at his ease,
for in the end good singing tires.

187.

Item: to the Captain of the Watch
I give two handsome little pages,
Filbert and Marquet, both a notch
in the Provost Marshall's belt for ages,
or most of theirs, and more like sages
for all the services they know.
If laid off now and no one engages
them then barefoot they must go.

188.

Item: to Chappelain I pass
my lowly cleric's chapel. True,
there's not much reading, a dry mass,
that's all it needs. I'd give him too
my cure but that would hardly do.
He doesn't like the care of souls
and hates confession but gets through
the maids and ladies, picking holes.

189.

Because he takes my meaning well,
to Jean de Calais comes this right
(though he's not seen me for a spell
of thirty years and never quite
recalls my name): if what I write
in my last will is hard to see
or difficult, let him shed light
and prune it like an apple-tree,

190.

or gloss, define and annotate;
transcribe, diminish, or augment;
cancel, suppress or regulate
by his own hand with my consent;
and if he cannot tell what's meant,
to make what sense of it he can
for better or worse to his content.
In all of this I trust the man.

191.

Should any here have passed from death
to life without my knowledge, I wish
the said Calais to see my breadth
of vision quite fulfilled and dish
my alms out to the pauperish.
But if he keeps them in his greed
I leave his conscience to swish
about him till he mends the deed.

192.

Item: I wish to be laid to rest
in St Avoye – no other place.
And so they see me at my best
(not in the flesh; what paint can trace)
I'll have my portrait, figure and face,
life-size in ink if it's no great
expense. A tomb? No, not the space,
besides, the floor won't bear the weight.

193.

Item: upon my grave, I think,
without embellishment, in large
letters, what follows. (If there's no ink,
carbon or coal will do my charge.)
Don't crack the plaster with a barge-
pole, take some care and let men see
the legend of me still at large,
of one who lived fool-heartily:

194.

EPITAPH

Here in this garret lies and sleeps
one whom love's arrows shot and killed,
a poor worthless scholar home for keeps,
named François Villon. He never tilled
a field nor ploughed his furrow. He willed
his all away: tables, beds, his bread
and baskets. Gallants with glass now filled
recite this verse for one now dead:

195.

RONDEAU

Grant him eternal rest now dead,
Oh lord, and everlasting light.
He wasn't worth the candle, quite,
or even a parsley sprig. His head
was shorn, his beard and eyebrows shed –
a turnip scraped and scoured white.
Grant him eternal rest now dead.

Strict justice banished him and sped
his arse up with a spade all right.
He cried: 'Appeal!' not subtle, quite.
God grant him eternal rest now dead.

196.

Item: I'd like someone to peal
the great bell – the one that's made
of glass – though everyone must feel,
hearing the sound, his heart's afraid
for it has warned of storm or raid
and saved rich soil in recent times.
Whether thunder or armed men invade
all evil ceases when it chimes.

197.

Four loaves the ringers shall receive
or half a dozen if four's too few,
(as much as that the rich don't leave!)
but rockcakes of St Stephen. Now who?
Volant is careful; he will do,
but come to think of it, his share
will last him for the whole week through.
The other? John the Guard is spare.

198.

To accomplish and achieve so much
I'll name executors below:
such men who have the business touch
and keep their debtors happy. You know
they're not the greatest boasters, though
they have the wherewithal, thank God.
They'll take full charge on the whole show.
I'll name you six: record this squad:

199.

Martin Bellefaye for one I name –
the Criminal Lieutenant. And two?
I've thought that out. I have a claim
on Sire Colombel, and if he knew
it would amuse him or accrue
something he would perform the task.
Third? Michel Jouvenal will do.
To take sole charge these three I'll ask.

200.

But if they make some poor excuse,
fearing the outlay, or point-blank
refuse, I therefore must induce
the following: all men of rank
and breeding: Philippe Brunel, I'll thank,
a noble squire, and next his neighbour,
Jacques Raguier, on him I bank;
and lastly Master James's favour.

201.

All three are good honourable men,
seeking salvation for their souls,
fearing the Lord their God. These then
would lose pocket, go in holes,
rather than not fulfil their rôles
in this my ordinance. There'll be
no other over them who controls
the way things go: they'll make quite free.

202.

But not a thing for the Probate Court,
but rather for a youngster priest,
Thomas Tricot. I'll drink a short
on him although it cost at least
my yard. To him when I've deceased
will come the rights to *Perrette's Hole;*
but only when his skill's increased
at tennis. Strokeplay has its rôle!

203.

Guillaume de Ru will be in charge
of all the funerary lamps.
For pall-bearers the choice is large:
my executors will choose.
Pain clamps
my groin, scalp, chin and brows. The cramps
come worse than they have ever done.[64]
I'm racked and pain upon me ramps –
Time to seek pardon from everyone.

204.

BALLADE.

To hermits, Carthusian or Celestine,
To Devotee and Friar – to heel,
servant, trim little piece and queen
who wear tunics and coats a deal
too tight; to lovesick fops who kneel

wearing their boots of yellow tan,
and never make complaint or squeal:
pardon I cry from every man.

To whores who let their tits be seen
to draw a larger clientele;
to brawlers, con-men on the scene,
to showmen with their apes at heel
to fools and those in farce who steal
away, whistling, six to the van;
to dolls on strings – in hand or real –
pardon I cry from every man.

Except those sons of bitches so mean
they made dry crusts my daily meal
and made me shit hard in between,
not three turds more now can I feel
though farts and belches I would peal
for them if sitting down I can.
And yet to end all rows for real:
pardon I cry from every man.

Let someone bang their ribs a deal
with good stout weighty mallets; fan
their heads with lead weights till they reel;
pardon I cry from every man!

205.

THE OTHER BALLADE.

Here ends at last the Testament
of poor Villon. When next you hear

the passing bell, you should lament
in loudest red behind the bier.[65]
He died of love, he made that clear
and swore it on his only ball –
disseminated love from here to here:
prepared to leave the world and all.

He spoke no lie, or never meant
to lie, I'm sure. It would appear
that spiteful girls of his had sent
him haring off in mad career
like a pot-stirrer till from here
to Rousillon, each bush and wall
sported a tatter of his gear:
prepared to leave the world and all.

Those are the facts of the event:
he died in rags. Further, I fear,
as he lay dying, almost spent,
love whipped him up again in sheer
pain from its buckle-tongue (and here
we register some doubt). In gall
and agony it cost him dear:
prepared to leave the world and all.

Prince, gentle as a merlin, hear
what next he did upon the pall:
he swigged his wine, dark red and clear,
prepared to leave the world and all.

THE END

OTHER POEMS

THE DEBATE BETWEEN VILLON'S HEART AND BODY

What's that?
It's only me.
But who?
Your heart.
I'm hanging on by just a single thread.
It saps my strength and nerve, you're so apart,
withdrawn – a corner-skulking mongrel, head
on paws. And why is this? Because you've led
a merry dance, my friend.
So what?
It's me
that takes the knocks, you know.
Oh let me be.
But why?
So I can think of a new line
to shoot.
How soon?
When childhood's over, see?
No further murmur then.
That suits me fine.

What's on your mind?
To play a nobler part.
You're thirty now – an age when mules are dead.
You call it childhood still?
No more, dear heart.
Madness it must be taking hold instead.

Of what? My collar, then?
Your empty head
knows nothing.
That's not quite true at all. I see
flies in the milk as plain as they can be:
one's black, one white.
Is that so, that the sign?
You want more argument?
You're lost.
Not me!
No further murmur then.
That suits me fine.

Mine the heartache, yours, the sorrow and smart.
If you had been some simple knucklehead
then I could sometimes take your silly part,
but fair or foul's all one, I would have said,
for all you care. You have a skull of bed-
rock or you choose the life of misery
rather than honour. Now answer that for me.
Once I am dead it's no concern of mine.
Some comfort that!
What noble oratory!
No further murmur then.
That suits me fine.

Where's the trouble?
Bad luck from the start.
When Saturn packed my bags for me he fed
the troubles in.
You're mad. You take the part
of serving man when you are lord instead.
Solomon writing in his scroll has said:

'A wise man has,' it goes, 'authority
over the planets' influence.'
Not so with me.
I'm as they made me. That's no creed of mine.
What's that you say?
That's my philosophy.
No further murmur then.
That suits me fine.

Very life you want?
God strengthen me.
It takes . . .
Well, what?
Repentance it must be,
Limitless reading.
Of what?
Philosophy,
Leaving all fools.
I'll see how I incline.
Okay, remember now.
My memory
Never fails.
Don't wait till worse, you see?
No further murmur then.
That suits me fine.

BALLADE: EPISTLE[1]

Have a care, take care of me!
my friends, at least, my friends – please.
I'm ditched, no holly hedge or tree
for shelter. Fate for once agrees
with God to exile me. I'll freeze.

My girls, you lovers, greenhorns, gay
dancers and pairs in the Antic Hey,
prickers of spurs and darts in air,
guzzlers whose gobs cascade with spray:
poor Villon, will you leave him there?

Singers of songs whose tongues make free,
dandies in words and deeds that please,
you bums without a franc or fee,
you wits so absent-minded – seize
the chance – he dies by slow degrees.
Makers of motet, sonnet, lay,
your wedding breakfasts won't convey
much warmth where winds nor lightnings dare:
thick walls blindfold his eyes from day:
poor Villon, will you leave him there?

His state you ought to come and see,
nobles who pay no loyalties
nor tax to lord or monarchy,
unless to Heaven. His fasts are these
days all the week: bread without cheese
washed down the water treatment way.
His teeth like a rake's rot and decay.
He lies on earth that's dank and bare,
no bed nor chair for him today:
poor Villon, will you leave him there?

Princes here named, the young or grey,
the king's pardon you could sway
to raise him back into the air
inside a basket. Pigs, they say,
will do as much for swine that stray:
poor Villon, will you leave him there?

QUATRAIN[2]

Francis I am, which weighs me down
born in Paris near Pontoise town,
and with a stretch of rope my pate
will learn for once my arse's weight.

VILLON'S EPITAPH[3]

Brothers that live when we are dead,
don't set yourselves against us too.
If you could pity us instead,
then God perhaps will pity you.
We five or six strung up to view.
dangling the flesh we fed so well,
are eaten piecemeal, rot and smell.
We bones in a fine dust shall fall.
So do not laugh us into Hell:
pray God may save us one and all.

Brothers, if that's the word we said,
it's no disparagement to you
although in justice we hang dead.
Yet all the same you know how few
are men of sense in all they do.
Pray now we're dead that Jesu's well
of grace shall not run dry – nor Hell
open in thunder as we fall.
We're dead; don't harry us as well:
pray God may save us one and all.

Showered and rinsed with rain, we dead
the sun has dried out black and blue.

Magpie and crow gouge out each head
for eyes and pluck the hairs. On view,
never at rest a moment or two,
winds blow us here or there a spell;
more pricked than a tailor's thumb could tell
we're needled by the birds. Don't fall
then for our brotherhood and cell:
pray God may save us one and all.

Prince, Lord of Men, oh keep us well
beyond the sovereignty of Hell.
Down there we'd make no business call.
No laughing matter I can tell:
pray God may save us one and all.

QUESTION TO THE CLERK AT THE GATE[4]

What do you think of my appeal,
Garnier? Was it right or wrong?
Every creature gives a squeal
before it's hurt and makes a song
and dance to save its skin. How long
then, when they lectured me to death
for their amusement, should I, strong
and silent, hold my bated breath?

I would have had a better deal
as heir of Hue Cappel (a long
line of butchers). Then, I feel,
no drop could ever touch my tongue
through cloth. You see? Don't get me wrong.

But when they sentenced me to death
and pulled a fast one, should I, strong
and silent, hold my bated breath?

Under my hat, you thought, the real
grey matter hardly could belong
to tell them all that I appeal.
There was, I promise you, headstrong
enough never to trust that throng.
So when they sentenced me to death
by hanging, should I have gone along
and, silent, hold my bated breath?

Prince, if I had lost my song
I'd be where Clotaire lies in death
or like a lookout, the drop long,
and, silent, hold my bated breath.

NOTES

I have not attempted in these notes to explain every allusion. With Villon, this would be an impossibly cumbersome task and a scholar's life work. This edition is intended as a reading one rather than an academic. I have therefore concentrated on cross-referencing the characters who appear in both the main works and noting the major decisions taken in translation. The stanzas are numbered for ease of reference, and for this purpose, ballades and rondeaux etc., are treated as one stanza or poem. Many stanzas in Villon are still open to interpretation and the reader can make his guess without being nudged by notes. A rule of thumb would be that if there is the ghost of a pun or an innuendo it was intended! A general point that may be made here is that the italicised names, such as *The Helmet*, are not pub-signs but house-signs used in Paris at this period.

NOTES TO 'THE LEGACY'

STANZA	NOTE	
1	1	I am virtually convinced that the inconclusive syntax of this stanza is a joking reflection upon 'mind and senses clear'. The opening line of the next stanza re-inforces this view. Vegetius was a fourth century Roman, author of *De Re Militari.*
2	2	As Pound has said Villon always rhymes on the definite word. Not much you can do about it in English, hence these assonances instead of full rhyme.
4	3	The allusion in the last line to ploughing is as much sexual as agricultural. I omit a similar innuendo concerning 'coining' for reasons of space and versification.
6	4	It seems to have been criminal investigations over the robbery of the College of Navarre as much as love that made Villon leaves Paris in haste.
10	5	You cannot always put a foreign author's puns in the right place. 'Relictuary' is a poor attempt to catch the flavour of several missing ones.
11	6	Ythier Marchant: a boyhood friend of Villon's, born of a wealthy family. He became important in Burgundian politics until bought off by Louis XI who hated him. Later he was involved in a plot to poison the king and finished up in the dungeons where he died in 1474. The sword Villon gives is a 'branc' which may pun on 'bran' meaning 'excrement'. Le Cornu was rich and worked in state finance and then as criminal clerk in the Châtelet. He died in 1476 of the plague.

STANZA	NOTE	
12	7	Saint Amant Villon hated. As clerk of the Treasury he had great influence. He seems to have been of poor mettle, sexless and dull. (See *The Testament*, stanza 105.)
12	8	Blarru was a goldsmith. The gift of a zebra is a puzzle – though I should think from its antics it had a sexual significance.
12	9	This refers to a papal decree of 1215 ordering all christians to confess with their parish priest once a year. Villon restores the decree for them out of his hatred for the Mendicants who had rights of hearing confession granted in 1449.
13	10	Robert Vallée: son of a family of rich financiers, he seems from this stupid and henpecked.
16	11	Jacques Cardon: a rich clothier in no need of gloves and capes.
17	12	Regnier de Montigny: born of an important family that had come down in the world, he turned early to crime and probably was the man who introduced Villon to the underworld. He was hanged in Paris in 1457. For Jean Raguier the only further information is in *The Testament*, stanza 113.
18	13	The Seigneur de Grigny, Philippe Brunel, was a truculent noble who tried to mend his fortune by robbing his own church for which he spent fourteen months in prison and set the law-court against him by his truculence in reply. The buildings bequeathed to him were ruins in Villon's time.
19	14	Jacques Raguier: possibly son of Charles VII's master cook – also from this a master drunk. There is a suggestion too that he was a master lecher – which I have hinted at in the pun on 'share' and 'plough-share'. (See note 3.)
20	15	Jean Mautaint was Examiner at the Châtelet. He investigated the robbery of the College of Navarre.

STANZA NOTE

Pierre Basanier: notary at the Châtelet.

Their lord was the Provost Robert d'Estouteville who seems to have taken an interest in Villon's case. As head of the police he was extremely powerful. (See *The Testament*, stanza 147–8.)

20 16 The lawyer is named in the French as Pierre Fournier; something had to give in the versification! He was not in fact Villon's lawyer but lawyer to the community of Saint-Benoît at the Châtelet.

21 17 Jean Trouvé was an assistant butcher; the gifts he is offered, though appropriate to his trade, suggest to me that he was not much use with women.

22 18 This particular Captain had his right to the post – dependent on one's nobility – challenged by someone who claimed his knighthood. Villon settles the question by giving him a mock knighthood.

'The Lily Pad' is as near as I can get to the pun in the original upon 'lis' and 'lit'. Beds would be welcome enough in prison. (See: *Epistle: To My Friends* in the miscellaneous poems.)

23 19 Perrenet Marchand: constable and bailiff at the Châtelet none too keen on law and order. The charge here is that he is also a whoremonger. Bales of straw were strewn in prostitutes' rooms as well as in dungeons.

24 20 Jean de Loup and Casin Cholet were crooked friends of Villon's. In 1456 they were employed, God knows how, as river guards on the Seine. They presumably took advantage of this for poaching and filching as described. Wood and charcoal were easy for them to come by from the ships and boats whose loads they were meant to guard.

STANZA	NOTE	
25–6	21	These men were old usurers of great wealth based mainly in salt supplies. 'Blanc' was a small silver coin; four would be worth about eight shillings or forty new pence. The 'delicate tasters' tries to capture the ambiguity of the French, meaning 'worms' as well as 'titbits'.
27–9	22	A similar sarcasm continues here. These two are both wealthy and old and influential. It is difficult not to see a suggestion of homosexuality here and a dildo in the crozier or cue – though either would undoubtedly like to have been bishop. Letters of nomination signified a graduate's fitness for a benefice and were, of course, untransferable.
30	23	Windows were valuable in those days and often bequeathed. Villon had none, but presumably the spider's web is of a similar pattern.
33	24	Jean de la Garde was a seller of spice. There is a sexual suggestion in the imagery of mortar and pestle, especially as several spices were thought to be aphrodisiac. (See *The Testament*, stanza 119; 181.) St Antony's Fire is now known as gangrenous erisipelas. For whom it was intended here is not known.
34	25	Pierre Merbeuf: a rich clothier. Nicolas Louvieux: a rich magistrate and tax-collector. The Prince of Fools: a sort of Festival figure who distributed cardboard coins along the streets in imitation of the King during processions.
35	26	The Bell was called Marie and could be heard all over Paris on a calm day. Villon's room was only about a hundred yards away from it. It rang curfew and angelus, mentioned here.
36–8	27	These stanzas mock Scholastic terms and philosophy. As for rhyming, I have left them much as they are.

STANZA	NOTE	
38	28	The poem ends with a suggestion of self-love and masturbation as a direct contrast to the falseness and failure of courtly love with which the poem opens.
40	29	I have telescoped two implications here. 'To eat no figs or dates' may be the literal meaning; it may also mean 'Who doesn't eat, shit or piss'.

NOTES TO 'THE TESTAMENT'

STANZA	NOTE	
1	1	Thibault d'Aussigny: bishop of Orleans. He had Villon locked in the dungeons for some misdemeanour. 'Blessing streets' refers to the blessing of the people lining the route of street processions.
2	2	There is a pun here on *serf* and *cerf* – difficult to render.
5	3	The Picards were an heretical sect which did not believe in prayer.
6	4	The *Deus Laudem*, seventh verse: 'Let his days be few and let another take his bishopric.' The Authorised Version differs from this translation.
7	5	King Louis XI who acceded in 1461. It was customary for prisoners to be released when the king made a progress through a town. Hence Villon's release from the dungeons of d'Aussigny's palace – and hence the rather overdone gratitude.

STANZA	NOTE	
9	6	St Martial; a bishop of Limoges; popular etymology had confused the issue by awarding him military virtues.
13	7	The town is Moulins, residence of the Duke of Bourbon. *Esperance*, device of the Bourbons, is here translated as *hope*. Other commentators identify the town symbolically as the City of God.
15	8	*The Romance of the Rose:* an extremely popular, long, allegorical poem of the late thirteenth and early fourteenth century, begun by Guillaume de Lorris and finished by Jean de Meung. Chaucer also draws upon it. The quotation is apparently from a prefatory poem *The Testament* which Villon may have seen affixed to the manuscript.
27	9	'Rejoice . . .' Ecclesiastes 11:9 'Childhood . . .' Ecclesiastes 11:10
28	10	'My days . . .' Job 7:6
30	11	Celestines and Carthusians are religious orders with a preference for the hermitical life. The reference to oyster-fishing is probably sexual but also comments on their rather unmonkish habits of dress and display.
34	12	This colloquial saying for changing the topic is literal here.
36	13	Jacques Coeur, one of the richest men in France, a financier who aided the French Government in the last days of the Hundred Years' War. He died in November 1456.
42	14	Flora: A famous Roman Courtesan. Archipiades: a blunder for Alcibiades who was in any case a man renowned for his beauty in the Middle Ages. Presumably Villon nodded off during some lecture and misheard it. Thais: an Athenian courtesan who followed Alexander into Egypt.

STANZA NOTE

Buridan: a famous Fourteenth century professor at the University of Paris, hero of a popular legend. The Queen of France and Navarre was supposed to invite students to her rooms overlooking the Seine, eat, dance and make love with them and then have them thrown into the Seine to die quietly. Buridan, disguised as a student, is supposed to have infiltrated her rooms in this way and, on being thrown into the Seine, he landed in a barge of hay prearranged to be there.

Blanche: Blanche de Castille, mother of Louis IX.

Bertha, Beatrice and Alice: heroines of *Henri de Metz*, a *chanson de geste*; the first, wife of Pepin le bref, and mother of Charlemagne.

Arembourg: heir to Maine and wife of Foulques d'Anjou, she died in 1126.

43 15 Callixtus III: pope from 1455 to 1458, Alfonso de Borgia, famous for preaching a crusade against the Turks.

Alfonso V: King of Aragon and Naples, a great warrior and patron of the arts. He died in 1458.

Charles, Duke of Bourbon, died in 1456.

Arthur III, Duke of Britanny and Constable of France, died in 1458.

Charles VII: King of France from 1422–1461.

James II: King of Scotland, killed in 1460, besieging Roxburgh Castle.

The King of Cyprus was Jean III de Lusignan. He died in 1458.

Ladislaus, King of Bohemia, died in 1457.

Du Guesclin, constable of France under Charles V, a hero in The Hundred Years' War, died in 1380.

The Dauphin d'Auvergne may be Beraud III who died in 1426. The Duke of Alençon 'lately slain' is by a nasty joke Jean II who was not dead but deprived of his lands and titles for treason. Possibly Jean I is intended; in which case he died at the battle of Agincourt.

The whole ballade is extremely ironic since all those mentioned, except in the envoi, died between the writing of *The Legacy* in 1456, and *The Testament* in 1461.

44 16 This ballade was written in what Villon thought was old French. I have here and there suggested this by use of archaic English poetic diction.

50 17 The Lovely Armouress was an actual whore whom Villon knew in her extreme old age before 1456. She had been favoured in youth by the powerful Nicolas d'Orgemont, son of Pierre d'Orgemont, the famous chancellor to Charles V. Nicolas d'Orgemont was a Canon of Notre-Dame and had her installed in one of the houses of the cloister. He was finally jailed for plotting against the King and died, oddly enough, in the dungeons of the Bishop of Meung.

The nick-name derives from the fact that an attempt to clear the streets of prostitutes had forced the girls to double as shop keepers. Their nick-names thus derive from their trade-cover.

When Robert Lowell made a version of this famous lament he remarked, 'I have dropped lines, moved lines, moved stanzas, changed images and altered metre and intent.' In my version, are the only places in this translation where I have consciously altered images to fall in with modern taste. I have done this to

STANZA	NOTE	
		preserve stanzas which Lowell cut – the catalogues of sexual attributes in youth and age – in order to give them greater variety and a more concrete impact. An obvious example is 57 where 'grape skins' is not out of Villon; in stanza 58 I have done something to tone down the repetitiousness.
58	18	This is the verse Pound alludes to in his *A B C of Reading* where he says Villon always rhymes on the definite word.
60	19	This Ballade makes use of the nick-names of prostitutes derived from their shop-keeping. I have tried to English them and indicate their suggestiveness at the same time. *The Testament* makes clear the imagery as you read on.
61	20	Fremin: most commentators agree that this scribe is a fictitious device.
69	21	It is virtually impossible to translate a double ballade into English at the same time as you maintain the rhyme-scheme. I have resorted to final assonance for most of the rhymes but the translation is still far from satisfactory in that the historic present has had to be used. It is chiefly interesting for the autobiographical detail. Much of the other detail is inaccurate, obscure, or the result of a buffooning sense of humour.
69	22	It is interesting to note that in the penultimate stanza Villon himself seems to have strayed from the rhyme-scheme. It seems to have been a custom for wedding guests to pummel each other playfully, saying 'Remember this wedding!'
78	23	Tacque Thibaud was a favourite of the Duc de Berry, hated for his oppression and debauchery, but the name is clearly used here as an insulting nickname for the Bishop of Orleans, d'Aussigny.

STANZA	NOTE	
78	24	'Chokepears' were (i) a fruit, (ii) a metaphor for bitterness, (iii) a torture device of metal, pear-shaped, which could be expanded by a screw after insertion in the victim's mouth. The reference to water combines the idea of bread and water and the water torture.
79	25	His lieutenant was Pierre Bourgoing. His official was Etienne Plaisance, hence the pun. Robert was most likely the executioner of Orleans.
82	26	Moreau was a seller of roast meats; Provins was a pastry cook, and Robin Turgis owner of *Pine Cone Inn* – all three the type to whom Villon would owe debts and thus his heirs!
93	27	*The Romance of the Devil's Fart*, probably about a student escapade with the house-signs of Paris, is an early work of Villon's now lost. Guy Tabary was a member of the gang that raided the College of Navarre. He is 'honest' because his blabbing let the cat out of the bag about the robbery.
95	28	Theophilus: hero of a legend popular then of of a man who sold his soul to the Devil in order to keep his job; a version of it appears in *Le Miracle de Theophile* by Rutebeuf.
96	29	'Rose' refers by metaphor to Villon's girl-friend. In the ballade, verse 100, she is named acrostically as 'Françoys'.
100	30	The second verse of the ballade names 'Marthe' acrostically. Presumably 'Françoys' was false and 'Marthe' might have been true!
101	31	For Ythier Marchant, see Notes to *The Legacy*, stanza 11.
103	32	For Jean Le Cornu, see Notes to *The Legacy*, stanza 11.
105	33	For Pierre St Amant, see Notes to *The Legacy*, stanza 12.
106	34	Sire Dennis Hesselin was a fiscal judge.

STANZA	NOTE	
108	35	Pierre Fournier was not Villon's personal lawyer but attorney to the community of Saint-Benoît at the Châtelet.
109	36	For Jacques Raguier, see Notes to *The Legacy*, stanza 19. Villon offers him four 'placques' in the original; they were Belgian coins of little worth. Taking a tip from *The Legacy*, I have freely translated them into the Elizabethan 'plackets'!
110	37	See Note to *The Legacy*, stanza 34, for these two.
112	38	This is a buffooning stanza throughout. He virtually gives the address of the two women. I have indicated this southern dialect by some English 'stage' dialect.
113	39	A cheese soufflé was slang for a punch in the face. I have used 'Côte de Maubué' to make joke clear: Maubué was a well-known water fountain near Bailly's.
114	40	Michault de Four: a tipstaff of the Châtelet, he took part in the inquiry into the College of Navarre robbery.
115	41	The Two Hundred and Twenty were virtually city police under the charge of the Provost. Villon gives the two of them a *cornete* which means both a silk or velvet band for the hat or the hangman's hemp noose. I have tried to convey the idea with 'chinstrap' and the English idiom.
116	42	For Perrenet Marchand, see Notes to *The Legacy*, stanza 23.
117–8	43	For Wolf and Cholet, see Notes to *The Legacy*, stanza 24.
119	44	The Woodsmith was probably another tipstaff. Ginger was regarded as an aphrodisiac.
120	45	John Riou was a furrier, chosen captain of the Hundred Archers which were a volunteer militia.

STANZA	NOTE	
122	46	Robert Trascaille: clerk to Jean le Picart, treasury counsellor to the King, later a tax collector, who had no shortage of gold, let alone bowls.
123	47	The abbess was Huguette du Hamel, more likely to initiate her novices into sex than religion. After strong disapproval from the church, she invested the abbey's money and absconded with her lover Master Baudes le Maitre with all the titles of the abbey.
128	48	The original 'caige vert', probably refers to a house-sign, but the 'cage' had an erotic meaning also which I suggest as well as I can in the pun 'bird'.
131	49	The gorget is slang for hangman's noose. There's not much that can be done about it in English. The stanza, as a whole, with its technical vocabulary, can't be done decently into verse.
135	50	Here, as in most places, the coinage is used for sexual suggestion. Punning throughout I've tried to equal the suggestiveness in English. The penultimate line is an anachronistic allusion to Falstaff and 'conjuring within the ring.'
137	51	'Ave salus, tibi decus' is part of a Latin hymn to Our Lady. But *saluts* and *écus* were coins. I indicate the puns by spelling. The *Donatus* also suggests 'giving'.
138	52	The Great Credo was a joke for long term credit which of course these money-lenders hated. See Notes to *The Legacy*, stanza 25. 'Flans' here translated '*mint*' meant both 'custards' and the 'blanks' used in coining. This was as near as I could get.
144	53	The riding boots are a reference to sexual intercourse. For 'Michault' see *The Testament*, stanza 97.
146	54	Thibaud was a name for a cuckold. I use an

STANZA	NOTE	
		Elizabethan anachronism to suggest this.
148	55	The ballade has Estouteville's wife's names acrostically. It should be read as coming from him – or as a Villonous joke! Estouteville apparently did all that was said of him in the previous stanza. See Notes to *The Legacy*: stanza 20; note 15.
152	56	This ballade is the most tedious piece of Villon. It is translated here for completeness but with every evidence of impatience as the rhymes show!
153	57	Franc Gontier was the hero of a popular poem praising the simple life. Villon who had suffered it of necessity had no time for such naivety.
156	58	My Lady obviously kept a brothel. In fact, its sign *Le Pet au Diable* (The Devil's Fart) was the subject of Villon's earlier, lost poem. See *The Testament*, stanza 93. The graveyards were likely to be the cemetery des Innocents described in stanzas 176–9, a popular place for prostitutes. The harridans of the Linen Market would give as much as they got as the following ballade suggests, one difficult to translate as it rhymes throughout on proper names more systematic than those of English.
170	59	Colin de Cayeux was implicated in the College of Navarre robbery with Villon. He escaped jurisdiction several times by benefit of clergy but was caught in Senlis and condemned by a secular court and hanged on September 26th 1460. Montpipeau and Rueil were slang terms for robbing and stealing.
175	60	These were the patients in a hospital for the blind. They had the right to beg on holidays in the cemetery des Innocents. They will need

STANZA	NOTE	
		to tell good skulls from bad, and, possibly, good prostitutes from poor.
180	61	St Dominic here symbolises the Inquisition and makes this stanza heavily sarcastic.
184	62	Alain Chartier, the poet, left for lovers in his *La Belle Dame sans Merci* the making of songs and ballades.
186	63	For this play on ducks and geese, compare *The Legacy*, stanza 16. It is interesting, also, to compare it with 'Galen might go shooe the Gander for any good he could doe' from 'The Unfortunate Traveller' by Thomas Nashe. Or more recently: 'Love likes a gander and adores a goose' from Theodore Roethke's 'I knew a Woman'.
203	64	These remarks on illness have led to the conjecture that Villon suffered from syphilis. Though highly probable, it cannot be ascertained. Some readers take *Ballade: To his Girl-friend*, stanza 100, as equally suggestive.
205	65	Red was the colour in which martyrs were mourned. It is a joke here for the martyr to love. See *The Legacy*, stanza 6.

OTHER POEMS

TITLE	NOTE	
BALLADE: EPISTLE	1	This epistle was most likely written during his imprisonment at Meung in the summer of 1461. Even here, Villon cannot resist taking several knocks at his friends.
QUATRAIN	2	This was composed in his imprisonment in the Châtelet towards the end of 1462. He had been arrested for a minor brawling incident with a papal scribe Ferrebouc who, unluckily, had influence. He was tortured and sentenced to be strangled and hanged. The

STANZA	NOTE
	second line makes Paris a village in the district of Pontoise, but, more seriously, hints that things would have been differently handled in Pontoise which comes under the king's direct jurisdiction, unlike Paris.
EPITAPH 3	This was written during the same imprisonment.
QUESTION TO THE CLERK AT THE GATE 4	Villon appealed against the sentence of death and parliament set the judgment aside. This ballade is addressed on his release to the gate-keeper of the Châtelet, a man not without previous convictions. Villon's sentence was commuted to banishment for ten years from Paris.

ACKNOWLEDGEMENTS

Parts and versions of this translation have appeared in *Agenda*, and formed the first *Agenda Edition* booklet. *The Ballade* of former beauties appeared in *P.E.N. Anthology*, edited by Peter Porter.

Also by Peter Dale
THE STORMS
MORTAL FIVE